CEKPA

A Memoir in Beaded Essays

Praise for *Cekpa: A Memoir in Beaded Essays*

"Altman refuses to sand down the jagged edges, instead holding them up to the light in this tremendous book, carefully setting piece after piece into place to tell her story of making and remaking family."
—Elissa Washuta, author of *White Magic*

"This memoir will remind you that—in spite of current evidence to the contrary—strong women continue to make the world."
—Pam Houston, author of *Deep Creek: Finding Hope in the High Country*

"Altman lets us in on a love letter to her two daughters, to her extended family, and to the land. We are endlessly fortunate to bear witness."
—Charlie J. Stephens, author of *A Wounded Deer Leaps Highest*

"Identity, family, genealogy, drug use, youth, belonging, culture, love, sex, growing up, and finding oneself fill this remarkable story of rediscovery, a story that so many Native people today experience in parallel paths."
—David G. Lewis, author of *Tribal Histories of the Willamette Valley*

"Altman's brave and beautiful memoir stakes its claim in the growing canon of lasting literature written by transracial adoptees."
—Erika Hayasaki, author of *Somewhere Sisters: A Story of Adoption, Identity and the Meaning of Family*

"We need more honest, complicated voices like this in order to more fully comprehend this largely unknown experience."
—Shannon Gibney, author of *The Girl I Am, Was, and Never Will Be*

"Raw, honest, and enlightening, Cekpa: A Memoir in Beaded Essays by Leah Altman is an emotionally charged collection of essays that transmutes childhood trauma and loss into enduring self-acceptance."
—Terra Trevor, author of *We Who Walk the Seven Ways: A Memoir*

"The generous intimacy of this memoir will make you feel that you've known Altman forever, rooting for her the whole way."
—Allison Larkin, author of *The People We Keep*

CEKPA

A Memoir in Beaded Essays

Leah Altman

Ooligan Press - Portland, Oregon

Cekpa: A Memoir in Beaded Essays

ISBN13: 9781947845602

Ooligan Press
Portland State University
Post Office Box 751, Portland, Oregon 97207
503.725.9748
ooligan@ooliganpress.pdx.edu
www.ooliganpress.com

Library of Congress Cataloging-in-Publication Data on file.

Cover illustration and design by Alexandra Devon
Interior design by Chrys Buckley

Printed in the United States of America

For my daughters.

Content Warning

The book you hold in your hands tells a story about my truth—the best and worst parts, the ugly and the beautiful—all mixed up in one narrative that makes me human. Telling it takes courage. There are discussions of child abuse and neglect, navigating abusive environments, self-harm, mental illness, and sexual assault. Please take care in your reading, and know when and how to engage and disengage as you see fit. Only you know your own battle wounds.

Table of Contents

Preface

When your great-grandmother is telling a good story, she makes creases in her napkin like an accordion. She's almost always at the dinner table, when she is most likely surrounded by family members on an occasion during which we are all gathered, like Christmas or a birthday, or just the general Friday night gathering. (A common phrase in our family: "Are we doing Friday night?")

In place of a napkin, any small bit of fabric will do. A piece of paper, even . . . a doily, one of the ones she tatted herself lifetimes ago and that cover every surface in her living room.

She pauses—a long, dramatic pause—until she has all of the attention in the room, looking down at her napkin or paper or doily humbly, and waits until every eye is on her, and then she begins.

Someone once told me they caught me doing the same thing in a work meeting and commented on how effective it was. They mistakenly thought it a cultural thing, because I'm Native American. More specifically, I am Lakota. Our family on my birth father's side is from Pine Ridge, South Dakota. Your great-grandmother—my grandma, your grandma Gigi's mom, my adoptive mom's mom—is not my blood relative.

That doesn't mean they aren't our family. It means that they chose us. In fact, they had to go out of their way to get us—they had to really, really want a baby. And that baby was me, your mama.

The Indian Child Welfare Act (ICWA) of 1978 was created in response to the high number of Native children who were being placed in non-Native foster and adoptive homes. According to the NICWA, it is estimated that 25–35 percent of all Native American children were removed from their Native American homes and placed into foster or adoptive care at the time the act was written, and 85 percent of those children were placed in non-Native homes, even when Native relatives were available and willing to foster or adopt.

When Native children are placed in non-Native homes, they often lose any kind of connection with their cultures. In fact, foster care and adoption have been criticized as the continuation of boarding school policies in the non-boarding school era. When Indigenous children are cut off from their cultures, they struggle, experiencing the effects of racism and loss of identity without truly understanding why. They are assimilated into mainstream culture, and tribal cultures continue their vanishing acts.

ICWA is known as the "gold standard" for child welfare policy involving Native children, designed to make every effort to keep Native children in Native families. ICWA contains guidance on how child welfare administrators and advocates should treat cases involving Native children, including more rigorous efforts to keep the child with their family, looking for placements within the extended family, and then, finally, only placing Native children with enrolled Native American parents.

That said, even though ICWA has now been in place for decades, out-of-home placement still occurs at a much higher rate for Native children than for any other race. For example, Native children are four times more likely to be removed from their homes than white children. There is more work to do.

Still, ICWA is followed more closely now than when it was first enacted. Now, the standard process involves these steps:

- Providing active efforts to keep the child with their family, rather than simply removing the child from their parents as a primary measure
- Identifying a placement that fits under the ICWA preference provisions

- Notifying the child's tribe and the child's parents of the child custody proceeding
- Working actively to involve the child's tribe and the child's parents in the proceedings

While the intentions behind the act were positive and hopeful, compliance on the behalf of caseworkers, courts, and families is spotty at best.

During the time I was placed in foster care and adoption, the law was still relatively new, and training was not well established. For that reason, my birth father and his family did not know I was adopted until well after the fact. The caseworkers and courts had not made "reasonable efforts," as outlined in the ICWA, to work with my birth father's family to try to establish and maintain a relationship with me. Furthermore, when I was adopted out, enrolling me in my tribe was not a consideration. In fact, my records were permanently sealed in court files in Colorado, and all identifying information about my birth family was redacted in my adoption records in Oregon, as well.

You are my daughters, Aurora and Acacia. As I begin this story, you are four and two. We live in Portland, Oregon, in the Pacific Northwest, where the smell of pine and rain mingle with the scent of wet concrete and cigarettes.

When you read this, you will be much older. I imagine gifting this to you when you are transitioning into womanhood, when you are questioning your identity, when you are pushing against me towards independence, seeking the answer to the question, "Who am I if not part of my mother?" But I write this to you as you are now, when I see your little faces looking up at me and think about your life from here and how important it is for you to know where you come from so that you know where you are going. I don't know how to communicate with a teenager yet as a mother.

In Lakota culture, when a baby is born, the mother makes two cekpas. A cekpa ("check-pah") is a leather bag made into a sort of amulet that holds a baby's umbilical cord, signifying the child's connection to the mother and the land they came from. A cekpa is a form of art that represents ceremonial culture and also incorporates an aspect of utilitarianism; most cekpas are beaded or otherwise designed based on the sex of the baby—lizards for boys and turtles for girls—and, while beautiful and delicate, they are meant to hold something important and then be buried, hidden away, stowed in the depths of a larger bag or a stack of pelts.

There is a dummy cekpa and a real one, and the real one is hidden. The dummy cekpa exists to distract bad spirits that would try to steal the real one. Babies who grow up without a cekpa, or whose cekpa is lost or stolen by bad spirits, will grow up without that connection, yearning for something they know is missing.

Lakotas are taught that we came from Wind Cave, that tricksters fooled us into leaving our home under the earth to come out into the light, even though we had everything we needed underground. Now we can't go back because we don't know how to live underground anymore. We have a special connection to the land because we came from it; we were a part of it, once, and we see ourselves as an extension of the land we come from.

I grew up without a cekpa, without a connection to my ancestors, to the land we came from. I had to work backwards to find it; I have spent my whole life following the broken threads of our family, weaving them together like Spider Woman to make our web—our story—whole again.

Just the other day, Aurora, you asked me why one of the delica beads in a pair of brick stitch earrings I made was off-color—bright red in a part of the design that should be turquoise. I told you that as a bead worker, I occasionally make mistakes, because I'm not perfect. Only Creator, the Great Spirit, the energy of this universe, God—whatever you call it—makes things perfectly, and even in perfection is seemingly imperfection. It was a big concept for a child of your age. What you caught onto was: Mommy is not perfect. And I'm glad you did! Because later on, when I made a mistake, you told me, "It's okay, Mom. Remember, you're not perfect." I laughed, thinking, *I did it to myself*, but now I'm glad you learned it. It's an important lesson.

Spider Woman is a trickster spirit, which means that part of her role in our traditional Lakota stories is to show us how not to be, and that imperfection is natural, human. We are not perfect. I am not perfect as your mother, but I am doing my best to show you how to be, even if it means showing you how not to be.

I hold Spider medicine, which is not only trickster medicine. Spider Woman is also a storyteller. I still find missing threads of our story every once in a while, threads I never knew were even there, following each to its source, pulling it taut and connecting it with the rest. And now I tell our story to you so you will help me hold the threads together, and then you'll hold them long after I am gone.

Origin Story

I was born "Baby Girl Blackfeather." My foster mother called me Colleen. My adoptive parents named me Leah, after the actress Lea Thompson (best known for her role as Lorraine Baines in the *Back to the Future* trilogy). Later in life, I learned yet a third name, one my birth mother called me secretly, in her mind—Raindance.

I was adopted by my mother (the one I was raised by) when I was a baby, four months old, just out of foster care. One of her favorite stories, my "alternative birth story," is the story about how I came to be their baby.

"We wanted you for so long!" she says, her hands to her chest. My mother's hands are not long, skinny piano hands, like she'd always wanted growing up. They are tough hands, working hands, nurse hands. Hands that have held the hands of strangers in comfort, grief, and joy, have bathed naked bodies and cleaned blood and shit and hair, have caught brand-new babies still covered in layers of biofilm.

She and my father tried to have a baby before, but she couldn't. Instead, she was a foster mother for several years, until she signed up to adopt a baby.

My mother relishes telling me over and over that she asked for, had planned for, a baby boy with blonde hair and "bright blue eyes" like my dad. Her best friend also applied for adoption at the same time and got her baby boy: my cousin Jasper, everything my mother wanted.

Instead, my parents got a call one day about a baby girl. Although my father can pass as white, with light skin and blue eyes, he is Navajo and enrolled in his tribe, so they had asked if my parents would consider adopting an Indian baby. The Indian Child Welfare Act had been passed less than a decade earlier and was designed to keep Indian children with Indian families. My soon-to-be parents responded that they would take any baby; they just wanted a healthy baby to love and raise as their own.

So when they got the call, they left right away on a plane to get me.

"You cried and cried," my mom says every time she tells the story, pushing her dark hair back behind her ear. "You kept nuzzling and digging into my chest, but I knew you knew I wasn't your foster mother." The adoption agent told my mother that my foster mother had a big, pillowy bosom, and that she held and rocked me most hours of the day to comfort me. My new mother did not have the full, soft chest I associated with love and comfort.

"You screamed on the plane all the way home, especially during the plane's descent, when your little ear canals filled with pressure and then released."

I grew up knowing I was adopted. It always surprised me when people asked me whether I had always known I was adopted. I couldn't imagine the possibility of my parents lying to me about something so significant. I couldn't imagine anyone's parents doing something like that. Because I had such close, generous, loving parents growing up, I thought that's just how all families were, how they should be. I was very lucky. Not every family is that way, I learned growing up. As I became an adult, I realized that my own wasn't even as perfect as I believed when I was a child. But that's a process you go through as a young adult. My hope for you, my dear girls, is that I can protect you from harsh realities, as my parents did while I was young, while also preparing you better to accept imperfections, to see the gritty beauty in life, as I learned to.

One of the first people to meet me just as I was getting off the plane was my Grandma Nali, my father's mother. What I found lacking in my new mother's skinny chest, Grandma Nali made up for in spades.

She wasn't always a big woman. I've seen photos of her from her wedding day, when she was only fifteen, with light skin, dark eyes, and hair curled in waves, petite and in a beautiful dress. She looked gorgeous and happy, hanging off the arm of my grandpa, her head tilted a bit towards his, a slight smile on her face, eyes cast downward, as if listening to sweet words being whispered in her ear.

She had a Betty Boop clock, ceramic ware, figurines, dish towels—you name it, she had it. That old photo of her on her wedding day reminded me of Betty Boop. She told me one time that she loved Betty Boop because Betty was a symbol of the "modern woman" in her time, one that was independent and free of restrictions, happy. Her life was not that way. From the moment she married, she was a wife and mother. I remember her yelling frequently at my grandpa that he had "ruined her life."

I used to tell people that my very first memory was of a drive by in the neighborhood I grew up in, in southeast Portland in an area coined "Felony Flats." In that memory, I am a little girl playing in our front yard. My dad built one of those big playsets—the good, solid ones, made out of mostly wood with metal and plastic components. The little yellow baby swing seat. Blue ropes. Red slide.

In my memory, I see a rusty gray car in the style of a Cadillac slowly rolling into my sightline on the left, passing our house, and then moving to the side of the house directly across the street from us. My mom called that house "the gang house."

My little brother, your Uncle Ben, toddles out in front of me, heading to the metal fence, the kind with the diamond shapes. He is wearing a white collared shirt and navy-blue pants. It is sunny.

I don't remember hearing gunshots. I do remember seeing my mom run from behind me to my right. I remember her jumping on my brother, covering him with her body, yelling at me, "Get down, GET DOWN!" I don't remember laying on the grass, but there is something, an imprint of a feeling of grass on my face and the taste of the earth in my mouth.

My mother doesn't like it when I talk about this. She says, "I don't remember." When I press her, she will admit there was a shooting, maybe more than one, but she doesn't remember being there.

That was my earliest memory until I had Aurora. We had a difficult time adjusting to the breastfeeding relationship, so I spent many hours walking and bouncing on a Pilates ball, with her in a carrier strapped to my chest. She cried if I stopped.

Eventually, we graduated to a regular rocking chair. And that's when I remembered.

I was rocking Aurora for hours and hours. I can't remember if she was teething or having one of those infamous "mental leaps," or whatever it was. Everything that happens in your life, Aurora, has always been a "big deal." You know exactly how she feels, all the time. She was like that even as a baby, and she wouldn't sleep—she just cried and screamed—if she was the least bit uncomfortable. So, I spent many, many hours in that rocking chair. If I stopped, she would stir, and I would panic— "No! Go back to sleep." I'd shush her, racing back to the rocking chair. Transferring her from my arms to her bed was impossible, so I rocked.

It was during one of these rocking sessions that I looked out the window, closing my eyes to the warm sun rays peeking through the blinds, that I had the most visceral memory of being rocked as a baby, my face stuffed into my grandma's chest. I can still feel it now, the exact tilt and *whoosh!* of the motion of that particular La-Z-Boy rocking chair, as her favorite show plays in the background, some old soap opera.

My heart aches with that memory of my grandma. Before she passed, we had a falling out. She used to say horrible things about my mother when I was younger.

I used to spend a month or so in the summer at my Aunt Gertrude's house in downtown Redmond so I could be with my cousins, Crystal and Violet. I adored Crystal; she was a year older than me, but she seemed so much more mature. Crystal bossed Violet and me around, as older cousins and sisters do. We were all afraid of their father, my Uncle Jerry.

My Uncle Jerry was abusive to Aunt Gertrude and Crystal and Violet. I believe Crystal took the brunt of it. She was always the one to stand up to her dad to take the heat off her sister and mother. The result is that Crystal was bitter and angry; so was her mom. They frequently talked shit about their family and friends in ways that made me uncomfortable. Gertrude spoke to Crystal more like a friend than a mother. I suppose they needed each other in a different way than an emotionally healthy family would.

Sometimes the shit talking would turn toward my family.

"You're a little uppity, just like your mom," my Aunt Gertrude would say when she was annoyed with me. "Your mom thinks her shit don't stink." Gertrude and Crystal were both short and squat, little chihuahuas with big barks and no bite. Jerry reminded me of a leprechaun; to this day, I distrust men with beards, beer bellies, and beady eyes.

One time, Jerry was so angry at Gertrude and Crystal as he drove us that he gunned his giant, white Suburban SUV up onto the sidewalk. We drove like that for a few moments, halfway on the sidewalk, halfway in the street, pedestrians dodging out of our way. He had Metallica blaring. I curled up in the backseat, covering my ears, wishing I was home, safe.

I have been known to spend one hundred dollars or more on a jukebox app nowadays in an effort to avoid hearing more than one heavy metal song in a row during pool league night. One part flex over men who remind me of him, one part survival.

My Grandma Nali moved from Portland when I was about ten and lived just blocks away from Crystal's family until she died. Sometimes she joined the shit talking against my mom.

"But you're not like her, dear," she said, patting my head. "You're a Gibson. You're one of us."

I wasn't sure if I wanted to be.

When I was a teenager, Grandma Nali invited my dad to a BBQ where his ex-girlfriend was the guest of honor; she made a point of not inviting my mother. I offered to go. I was mostly interested in seeing who this ex-girlfriend was.

I cannot for the life of me remember the ex-girlfriend's name. Let's call her Linda. She was nothing, a frumpy, mousy thing with no personality. All I remember is that she had long, gray-blonde hair, glasses, and looked very uncomfortable. There were no sparks between her and my father. He avoided her and talked to my uncles all evening. I went home and told my mom she had nothing to worry about.

A few years later, in my twenties, my Grandma Nali called me while I was on a break at work and started complaining about my mom again. I felt something like anxiety filling up inside of me, and all of a sudden, I burst.

"Don't talk about my mom like that." I felt nervous, but my voice was clear and final.

"What?" she said, her voice full of surprise, a little lilt at the end. "What did you just say to me?"

"You know." I dug in deeper. "You're going to die an old, unhappy woman with no one to love you if you keep treating everyone this way."

She hung up on me.

She called back shortly later with my aunts and cousin in the background.

"Hi, honey," she said, her sugary voice dripping with sarcasm. "I just wanted to call to tell you how sorry I am that we argued." In the background, my aunts and cousins hurled insults like "you stupid slut," "fucking bitch," and "you are nothing."

For years afterwards, until she died, she called me drunk at all hours of the day and night. I made no effort to see her. I have no other memories of seeing her in person—just those drunken phone calls.

When she died, my family and my husband went to help go through her things and mourn. By the time we got there, my cousins and aunt were going through all of her jewelry and makeup. They had already gone through everything else. They refused to speak to us as they picked through her belongings like vultures. I walked out of the house and got in the car, saying I wanted to go to the hotel and eat dinner.

"Do you want to pick out anything for yourself, honey?" asked my father, worry lines creasing his forehead.

"No," I said as I got into the car. "I'm not going to fight over her things."

The truth, I realized, was that nothing physical was going to ease the ache in my heart for my Nali, my paternal Navajo grandmother, the woman who gave me a safe landing straight from foster care into her arms, who rocked me for hours until I felt safe. Fighting with them wasn't going to bring her back. It wouldn't give me more time with her to make things right between us, or make her a kinder, more loving person—someone I could connect with in my adult years, who was mature enough to hold her tongue about her daughter-in-law around her granddaughter.

When I got home, I remembered the necklace she gave me, with the little beaded Navajo girl hanging from the end, and the beaded moccasins that fit me perfectly. She gave me those things, long before she died, gifted directly and intentionally from her to me.

I have saved these things for you, my daughters, in a box in the storage space above my dresser in my bedroom, along with mementos from your father's mother and other items from my childhood. They are in the same box where I keep your cekpas.

Ice Cream Sundae

I remember when I first realized I was different from my adoptive family.

Grandma and Grandpa Schröder, my mom's parents, had a big, in-ground pool in their half-acre backyard. Growing up, we were the luckiest kids. Your Uncle Ben and I would swim all day at the pool.

No matter how long I laid in the sun with my books, I never got as brown as my brother. When I think of Uncle Ben as a kid at the pool, I see him always moving, jumping, running, diving, splashing. He had to hold his nose when he jumped or dived because he moved so much, even in the water, that he was constantly getting water up his nose.

Even though I didn't turn as brown as Ben, all my girl cousins and friends remarked about how well I tanned, that they wished they could tan like that. I never thought anything of it, until Jessica came over.

Jessica was my cousin Becky's best friend from church. Becky is Ben's age, so a few years younger than me. Becky and I were far enough apart in age that we weren't super close growing up, but close enough in age that we played together when we were around each other, which was quite often during the summer because of the pool. I knew Jessica from church, also, but this was the first time I remember her coming to Grandma's pool.

When you're in the pool, you notice bodies more, because of tight-fitting swimsuits and the way the sun bleaches your hair and darkens your skin throughout the day while you play. Kids are more physical in the water, too, splashing and dunking, somersaulting over each other and swimming under each other, playing Shark and Fishy Out of the Water.

There was a lip around the pool, about three feet down, where we could stand around the edge before it dropped off. At the shallow end, we could touch to about the mid-point, where the deep end began and increased to six feet in the deepest part of the pool (about three-fourths of the way to the end).

Becky, Jessica, and I were standing on the lip, about mid-way to the deep end, holding onto the edge of the patio that surrounded the pool, which jutted out a few inches over the water. We were talking, I can't remember about what.

I remember looking down at our arms and thinking how beautiful they were, Becky's fine white skin, like porcelain; my deep, sun-kissed tan; and Jessica's dark, rich black skin that was a novelty to me, something I didn't see very often in a family of Germans.

"Look!" I exclaimed, pointing to each arm in turn. "Becky is the ice cream, I am the caramel, and Jessica is the chocolate. We are a sundae!" My mouth watered as we all stared down at our arms, glistening with glittery chlorinated water.

It was a long pause, full of little-girl realizations. We were different. But we were all still beautiful. Long before anyone told us otherwise.

And then someone splashed someone, and we let go of the edge and swam away.

Back then, we had to drive to Grandma Schröder's from Felony Flats to use the pool. I remember driving home after dark each weekend after visiting Grandma and my aunts, who all lived on one street together, my hair still wet and slightly crunchy from the chlorine, my skin stiff from the sun. I yawned as I watched the moon out the backseat window.

"Mom, Mom! The moon is following us again!" I'd watch in wonder as the moon, in its various stages of fullness, seemed to float alongside us. I never remember getting to our destination.

Those days always seemed so safe to me, so happy and loving. I hope that's how you feel growing up, too. Aurora just recently started noticing the moon following us home from Portland to where we live now, away from the city, in the dark countryside next to the water.

By the time you read this, you'll be old enough to understand the things I'm about to tell you. I imagine giving this book to you when you are in that soul-searching, coming-of-age, heartbreaking time of your life when you need to know that there is nothing wrong with you, life is hard sometimes, and nothing is perfect, not even your parents.

I went to a private Catholic school from kindergarten to third grade, where obedience and excellence in academics were rewarded and disobedience and lack of productivity were punished. As the older child in my adoptive family, I sought the approval of my parents and teachers, particularly my mother, so I excelled.

Even early on, there was something about me, something missing inside the core of me, that drove me towards success. I always felt, even as a child, that productivity and approval equaled love. If I slacked at all, I feared that I was unworthy.

Even in my baby photos, I hardly ever smiled. I had full Indian cheeks with high cheekbones, like Acacia (who is currently three years old and with cheeks that rival even mine at her age). Unlike Acacia, every photo I have of myself shows a serious little baby with a perpetual pout. When I turned eighteen, Grandma Nali gave me the baby book she had kept for me with all my baby photos and photos of myself as a child, up to age eleven or so. Across the front in black Sharpie is scrawled, "Leah's cute book."

Even as young as first grade, I remember having terrible stomachaches whenever I had to go to school. I have a strong memory of pulling up to the school gate in my mother's car, seeing the chain-link fence and the line of my friends in their white and navy blue uniforms waiting to walk into class, and bursting into tears. I begged my mom to let me stay home. I refused to get out of the car. I threw up. She took me home.

At the end of each year from first grade to third grade, they created an award just for me at the end-of-year party: the kid to miss the most days and still get straight As.

By my fourth grade year, Uncle Ben had been diagnosed with ADHD, and my mom decided to start homeschooling us.

Uncle Ben still struggled, but I was so much happier. Computers were a novelty back then, and I remember our big box DOS machine and the homeschool programs my mom bought us. I raced through mine each morning and spent the rest of the day playing outside and reading books I took home from the library weekly I was in heaven. I skipped three grades and had to be held back from skipping more by the time we moved to Grandma Schröder's street.

That's when I started middle school, and things started getting hard.

During the time we were homeschooled, we moved to Parkrose, a neighborhood in Portland east of Interstate 205, in an area that was once farmland. The lots were on parcels; my grandparents—my mother's parents—owned two lots, one of which was split into two for my Aunt Terri's lot and my Aunt Dayna's lot, behind her. My grandparents lived across the street from my aunts. Our lot was two houses down a dead-end street from my grandparents.

I loved our huge yard and, once I completed my online lessons, I ran around it barefoot most days. I had free rein of the neighborhood, since most of it was made up of my family. I rarely went to a store or restaurant, so I hardly ever wore shoes. I remember running on hot concrete and bark dust down to my grandparents' in-ground pool, pulling slivers out of my feet before bed.

I did have to wear shoes to the library, so I pulled on my flip flops and hopped in the car when my mom took her weekly trip to pick out a couple romance novels. Midland Library was less than five minutes away driving.

I still remember how it smelled when the automatic doors would *whoosh* open—ink and old paper. That feeling from being outside in the sun and suddenly inside with air conditioning and track lighting. Midland Library was a newer building; the bathrooms were nice and clean. That was usually my first stop before exploring the stacks—I didn't want to have to stop and drop off my books at the front desk and lose my spot in the rows of books. I liked to browse alphabetically (still do), beginning in literature, then poetry, then mystery, then spirituality, then wherever my intuition took me. I always came out with stacks of books, sometimes ten or more books in a visit. I rarely finished all those books by the due date, racking up fines twenty-five cents at a time. When I turned eighteen, Grandma Schröder paid the one hundred dollar library fine I had racked up all those years.

My favorite thing to do when I was homeschooled, after I finished my schoolwork, was to climb up the tree in my grandma's yard to the branch with the best dip in it for lounging and to read surrounded by cedar boughs. I watched as neighbors and family members walked below, listening in to their conversations. I named every tree in my grandma's yard. The reading tree was named Progeniskis after a character in *A Wrinkle in Time.*

By what would have been my sixth grade year, I tested two years ahead. It would have been three years, but I couldn't show how I was able to get the multiplication answers correct, so they weren't sure if I was doing it the right way. My parents were worried about my ability to keep up socially in middle school, so they only let me attend a year ahead—meaning I skipped sixth grade and started school in seventh.

Once again , just as before I was homeschooled, I did really well academically, but failed socially. I skipped as many days as I possibly could without getting kicked out or left behind. When I was in school, speaking and being around others was excruciating. It pained me to be in the presence of other people. I was critical and fearful of every move I made. I felt like I couldn't breathe when people were looking at me.

> "Why don't you smile more?"
> "Why are you so quiet?
> "Are you okay?"
> "You look so serious."
> *No, I'm fine. This is just my face.*

Self-Medication

The needle goes in and out of flesh.

As it enters and exits the spongy skin, it disperses flowy ink in blood red. This is the inside of the butterfly, various ruby tones encircled by black lines.

My body reverberates from the skin to the bones, the tremors traveling up my left arm into my jaw, rattling my teeth. The vibration sets into my layers of tissue and sinew and bone. The pain doesn't feel like pain anymore. I breathe with it, through it.

It becomes a part of me.

I am fourteen. A girl. A girl at fourteen with memories of shadows and a door closing, ghosts that visit me at night and press against my body. Sometimes I wake up in palpable fear, not breathing, afraid that taking a breath will alert the phantom to my presence.

I collect razor blades. My mom's razors are single blades, cheap, made for quick leg-smoothing touch ups. But my father's are the best—I love when I find quadruple blades. They are always the smoothest and sharpest, made for rough whiskers. I think of my dad's whiskers when he kisses my face, prickly at the end of the day.

I pull apart the plastic encasing the blades, tearing them open where the plastic is fused into the holes. Sometimes I get nicks when I do this; I suck my knuckles and fingertips. My blood tastes like metal, like putting a penny into my mouth.

I once read an article about animals in the wild. Some species, like big cats in Africa, rub themselves against trees and rocks until their skin bleeds when close members of their pack die. The endorphin rush from self-mutilation soothes their grief. They are self-medicating.

When I think about that, I don't feel so fucked up.

I don't cut to die. I know how to do it, but I purposely don't make the deep "cross of death" on my arms. I prefer my left arm. I prefer light, feathered cuts. My mom's razors are actually the best for this, because they are more rough, less sharp, and they cause more jagged ripping than my dad's.

When I'm done, I lick my arm clean, like a cat.

I go to the bathroom, where my mom, who is a nurse, stores medical gauze and tape. I know how to wrap my arms like she would at work. I wash my arms with soap and water and wrap them. I wear a hoodie with long sleeves the next week at school. It is approximately seventy degrees.

At school, I don't eat much. Instead, I drink Slimfast shakes and fries from the lunchroom with extra seasoning and ketchup. At home, my favorite snack is raw carrots dipped in honey and a cheese stick. I don't eat breakfast.

When I was ten, my mom told me I have to be careful about my weight, being Native American and all. I checked out a book about yoga from the library and taught myself how to meditate. I was already a vegetarian—I hated the texture of meat. I felt I could taste the fear of the animal when it died.

I became obsessed with the idea of Buddhist monks who live up in the mountains, meditating and living off of air. Really—they don't eat, but they survive. They barely move. I find ways to get out of exercising during PE at school.

Controlling my weight makes me feel strong. With every pound I lose, I feel more beautiful. Grown men follow me around the mall, asking for my number. I feel powerful.

One day, my mother gets up from work, and I jump up from the couch to hug her. I've had a bad day, sitting alone with my depression like a wet, scared cat curled on my chest. As I reach out to touch her, everything becomes fuzzy at the edges, and then black. I wake up on the floor.

Twenty-two years later, I watch the needle and ink traverse the roadmap of pink lines across my skin. Aurora's middle name is Kimimila—"butterfly" in Lakota. Acacia is named after a Persian tree that can grow in the most untenable conditions, like in the hot desert. There are seven butterflies covering the scars on my left arm, and one long acacia tree branch winds its way through them, wrapping itself around raised lines.

I lay back as my brain floods with adrenaline and endorphins and serotonin, taking deep breaths and relaxing, rolling with the pain.

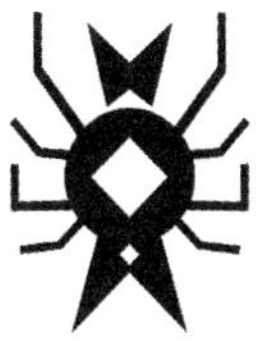

Fifteen

I am fifteen. Fifteen is when I stopped starving myself and started loving my curves, loving what my body could do, loving myself, maybe too much. Fifteen is a cotton candy girl with pink and purple hair unknowingly infatuated with the skate guard at Oaks Park ten years before I knew I loved him. Fifteen is when I cheated on a boy who loved me, who I didn't love. The boy I cheated with held me so gently all night and then told me not to expect anything from him when we woke up the next morning. Fifteen is sun and hot dogs and roller coasters and glitter and painting ourselves in our bikinis and running down the block in the rain and stamping in the puddles rinsing off paint in colorful rivers down the drain staining the bathtub gray and hot pink and blue. Fifteen is before I knew a broken heart. Fifteen is when we saved baby kittens, crawling through the roof of a tiny shack to rescue and raise them. Fifteen, I learned about grief when I found one of the baby kittens dead underneath my bed, not knowing how he died. Fifteen is a chaotic beautiful rainbow acid sky and girls on the cusp of becoming women, running wild and savage, angry, powerful, free.

Almost a Car Crash

I was flying up the freeway in my little 1992 Nissan Sentra hatchback. The windows were rolled down, and it was a beautiful spring day. The cool air felt good on my hot skin.

The Nissan was my very first car. I picked it out when I saw it sitting outside one of my favorite little bookstores in southeast Portland near Cleveland High School less than a year earlier. It had a sign on it that read "$1,000 OBO." My dad bought it outright, a grand in cash, for my sixteenth birthday. He didn't believe in negotiating.

He took me to a parking lot right after we bought it, down the street at the old K-Mart. The gigantic parking lot, bigger than a football field, was mostly empty. He showed me how to drive stick; I cried and cried, because I was so frustrated. And then suddenly, it clicked.

About ten months later, accelerating on the freeway, the wind blew my long hair around my face. It tangled in clumps when it mixed with my thick, salty tears. I kept thinking, *just make it until you get home. You can hold it together until then, can't you?*

My first high school, Parkrose High School, hadn't worked out. I started the school in honors classes and soccer, and quickly dropped out because of skipping classes. I also got caught smoking pot in the parking lot with the "bad kids" before soccer practice. My childhood anxiety and PTSD had transformed into drug and alcohol abuse.

The drugs and alcohol led to more anxiety, and acting out, and then more trouble.

After dropping out of school, I felt useless and isolated and unloved. I lined up fifty-six ibuprofen and aspirin and Tylenol and took them all at once. My Grandma Schröder had me drink liquid charcoal to throw it all up, and my parents made me walk around all night to make sure it was out of my system before I could sleep.

After that failed attempt, I tried again and landed myself in the psych ward of the hospital. While I was in the hospital, I gravitated to art therapy. My pastel drawings were nightmarish, but I loved them. I brought them home and kept them taped to my closet door. My roommate was a girl who OD'd on acid and woke up screaming every night, thinking that her room was filling with blood. One night, a girl tied a cord from her window blinds around her neck, covered it with her hair, and sat down calmly in front of the other patients watching TV until she passed out. Seeing other youth in the throes of intense mental illness helped me find the resilience I needed to heal.

After my stint in the hospital, my alcohol and drug addictions landed me in an outpatient drug treatment program for youth. On my last day of the drug treatment program, they kicked me out for bringing a pizza to celebrate, saying that I could have dosed the pizza. I threw it at the counselor and walked out.

I felt like even drugs, alcohol, and cutting had failed me. Trying so hard to be a "bad kid" didn't really get me anywhere more than trying to be a "good kid" did. Nothing changed. I still struggled with anxiety and depression. I felt hopeless. I kept drinking and using. My parents were worried about my influence on my little brother (Uncle Ben) and told me that if I didn't stop drinking and using and acting out, I would have to leave.

The day I left home, my dad and I were fighting. I can't remember why, but I'm sure it had something to do with my habit of refilling his vodka bottles with water after drinking about a quarter out of each. Or when I found a brick of my parents' pot in their bathroom and took a few buds, a little bit every day, and sold it to the kids at school. Or it could have been about me sneaking out at night; he screwed my window screen in so I couldn't open it anymore, so I simply cut the screen open with a knife.

I don't remember much about the fight, but I remember flipping my dad off and yelling "Fuck you!" as I walked off down the driveway. He looked shocked, confused, and worried, more than anything.

After the fight with my dad, I stayed away from home for about six months, crashing on friends' couches and even hooking up with the leader of a street gang, living in squats and tents and even a car for about a month in the woods.

One day, I was walking through Saturday Market on the west waterfront, and I ran into my parents.

"Honey, are you okay?" asked my mom. "We've been worried sick." She furrowed her forehead. My dad stayed quiet, but also looked worried.

"I'm fine," I said. "But I found out that you guys put a runaway report on me. You know that's not exactly how it happened. You told me to leave, so I left." I turned and walked away as my parents tried to explain.

At the time, that's how I felt. It seemed straightforward to me. I didn't understand that, as a parent, sometimes you are grasping at straws and make threats you don't really mean because you feel like you have no control over keeping your child safe. I already understand that now, even though you girls are still very young. Even as toddlers, you've proven that I don't always have control, even though all I really want is to keep you safe.

When the gang leader and I split, I went to live with Grandma Nali. She worked as a lunch lady at Cleveland High School, where she said that "the kids are a lot like me, with rainbow-colored hair and that weird rave music."

I did alright at Cleveland until 9/11. The kids at school started beating up on the Middle Eastern kids. I was only a quarter Persian, but they knew. I walked into my theater class the morning after the towers fell, and a girl I considered a friend turned to me, pointed, and said accusingly, "Leah is Middle Eastern." The entire class eyed me down. I turned around and walked out, never stepping foot again in that school.

Instead, a couple party friends and I started going to an alternative school in North Portland called Open Meadow. We had a great time there with the other raver kids. I never popped Molly, but I babysat the kids that did. Instead, I drank and smoked a lot of pot and drove us to parties in the woods and raves in abandoned warehouses in the middle of nowhere. My best friend, Katie, and I dressed in outrageous, highlighter-colored rave gear and glitter and lost ourselves in the bass we could feel in our throats. Music and drugs and booze made everything bad disappear.

Open Meadow had a strict three-strikes-and-you're-out policy. My commute was about an hour each way in rush-hour traffic, and sometimes, it took longer than I expected. The teachers frequently made allowances for my tardiness and did not report me as long as I wasn't too late; however, the few times I was fifteen or twenty minutes late to school, my absence was too obvious for them to turn a blind eye.

Despite the distance, I loved that school. It would have been easier to find a school closer to me, but I was willing to drive there for the experience and for my new friends. I was in the Corps Restoring the Urban Environment cohort; we explored wetlands and tracked them via GIS. I spent most of my days out in nature. They even arranged outings and experiences, like an overnight snow-shoeing trip on Mt. Hood.

On my last day of school at Open Meadow, the principal called me into the office. His name was Wesley. He sat me down and gently, yet firmly, explained that he couldn't make allowances for me over the other kids in the program. He told me I had to leave, without even telling my friends or the teacher goodbye. Just like that, everything I really enjoyed about my life was gone.

About twenty minutes after leaving Open Meadow, after Wesley kicked me out, I tapped the ash from my cigarette, my hand stuck out the window. A tear from my eyelid caught in the wind and splashed onto the burning tip, putting it out.

"Fuck!" I yelled out the window, throwing my cigarette. *Who cares about the environment?* I thought. *I don't even want to be alive anymore.*

I stared at the retaining wall two lanes over to the right.

I could just smash my car into that wall over there. Nobody would even care.

There was a deep urge in me to do it. That urge scared me. I felt compelled, almost like something outside of me was pressuring me to do it. I sobbed, tears streaming down my face. The speedometer creeped up to 80 mph—a lot for that little car.

I was crying so hard I couldn't see clearly. Everything was blurry. I was vaguely aware my situation was becoming more and more dangerous, more and more reckless. But it didn't feel real in that mindstate . . . everything felt dreamlike, hazy.

HONK! Honk, honk. I was starting to drift into the lane next to me.

I breathed in sharply and righted my car, slowing down slightly. I looked over at the driver in the car to my right, who had honked his horn.

He was handsome, a little older than me. He raised his hand and waved, concern on his face. *Are you okay?* He mouthed, motioning to his own face.

I took a sharp breath in, nodded, and then stared ahead, my face burning. I wiped away my tears, pulled myself together, and drove on.

All it took was a stranger.

After partying away three years of high school, I finally felt like I had had enough, but I didn't know where to go from there. I was so far behind, and I didn't know how I would ever make it up. No matter how much I drank or cut or smoked or popped, I never felt better after the high wore off. Everything just got worse, more difficult, and I just got further and further behind.

When you're a teenager and your life is out of control, it's so easy to give up. It was during that time that I found a gun in my grandfather's room. I put it in my mouth and imagined pulling the trigger. I kept thinking of my family, and how they would suffer due to my selfish act if I followed through. I suppose that's why I never actually made it through any of those suicide attempts. Something in me felt too guilty. And something in me wanted to believe there was a reason to live.

It's a really good thing I didn't pull the trigger. I found out later it was just a BB gun. I might have ended up paralyzed instead of dead.

Apple

I had to pee. That's the thing about ceremony. Every one of our ceremonies takes forever, and I have a tiny bladder. There is always a lot of coffee available, which makes me thirstier, too. Our ceremonies are usually out in nature or someone's backyard. So I am accustomed to peeing in the woods. Even now, as a mother and career woman, I would rather pee behind a tree or bush than any outhouse.

They say you're only safe "inside the circle" when you're in ceremony. This is accurate for just about any ceremony. (And because I know many readers will ask: "They" is anyone who will tell you they are the authority in such ceremony. It's an amorphous "they.") Because of the small bladder and the late nights and the coffee and the water, I end up leaving the circle a lot, which is dangerous. Particularly during peyote meetings.

The first time I was attacked by a spirit during a peyote meeting when I had to pee, I passed out. I was only vaguely aware of someone carrying me back into the tipi, walking me around the circle, and depositing me in front of the fire. My cousin told me after the ceremony that they fanned me down and prayed over me for an hour.

I remember being in some type of flat, dark place, where the ground kept shifting. There was someone there with me; maybe two someones. It was almost like a box—there was no way out. I was trapped. I could hear the people in the ceremony, in this world. But I was trapped in a dark place I couldn't leave, with strange spirits.

I woke up a couple hours later and motioned for the bucket. There was music and praying. I threw up, and then I felt better than ever, sitting up high on my knees and singing and praying with new vigor. They said I was lucky to come back. Some people don't.

The second time I was attacked by a spirit was the time I had to pee just before dawn, in the black of night. I was trying to wait for the light, but I had held it as long as I could.

The tipi was set up next to a creek. I headed over to it, feeling safest next to the water. I pulled my underwear down and my skirt up and released.

Drip-drying, I noticed a movement in front of me and looked up. At first, I couldn't make it out, a blue-black against the black night. It had horns and dark red eyes and a boxy head. It noticed me at the same time I noticed it. I pulled up my chonies and ran. This time, I made it back to the tipi before anything bad happened. However, we didn't leave the tipi for several more hours, well into the morning, because we could hear growling all around the tipi.

My cousin Sage is the one who got me into peyote ceremonies. Sage is from Tacoma, but he moved with his mom, my aunt, to Portland around the time I met him. We were both in sobriety, and we met at Portland Community College in the United Tribes club.

There was a high school counselor at one of the schools I dropped out of that I felt particularly drawn to, a woman I trusted. When I got kicked out of Open Meadow in what would have been my junior year, I went back to Cleveland to see her. I remember feeling hopeless, at my wit's end, not knowing what else I could do to finish school.

She didn't seem hopeful at first, but then she remembered hearing something about a new program called Collegebound—now called Gateway to College. It required that the prospective student have less than six high school credits (totally nailed that), and it paired each student with a college counselor to help them navigate the challenges of being a first-generation college student. Each student was a part of a cohort of other "at-risk" high school youth that were taking college courses for dual (high school and college) credit. Everything was paid for, and they even paid for transportation and book costs, too.

"It's basically handing you your high school and college degrees on a silver platter," she said. I couldn't fuck this one up. It was my last chance.

I liked the program much better than high school. After the first couple of trimesters, during which we only took classes in our cohort, we were let loose into regular courses with the mainstream students—the only difference was that we were younger and getting both high school and college credits.

I thrived on being in classes with actual adults, people who were really there to learn and excited about it. I joined multiple student groups, got involved in student government, and started drumming and singing with a Native drum group through United Tribes. I met Sage and a woman named Rose who invited me to peyote meetings and my first sweat lodge ceremony.

As I started going to Native ceremonies, I got to know a strong group of spiritual people who "walked the Red Road." Being around other Native people who were clean and sober encouraged me to quit drinking and using. I started supporting Rose at her annual sun dance ceremony and attending others in Oregon and South Dakota.

I moved back home with my parents when I started school at Open Meadow and was still living with them while I was attending Gateway to College. They were thrilled at my radical transformation and my sobriety. They used to take me to powwows when I was a kid, but they didn't really know how to connect me with other Native families in Portland, as my father hadn't tried to seek out that part of his identity. My Grandma Nali told me that she was taught not to acknowledge their Native heritage, to always claim and act like she was white for survival. For that reason, my father didn't know much about his Dine (Navajo) heritage or family.

Despite their lack of knowledge about our Native cultures, my adoptive parents always encouraged my participation in any activities they could find that related to Native heritage. When I turned to Native ceremonies for a connection as a teenager, my parents were supportive—and relieved.

One of the elders who hung around United Tribes and took my cousin and me to AA meetings and peyote meetings alike was named Jeremiah. He dressed like an old fifties rockabilly—slicked-back hair, smoker's voice, black leather vest and the white tee with the sleeves rolled up—the whole bit.

I was very proud of getting back into school and going to college. Sage and I probably both came off as arrogant, particularly around Native folks who hadn't had the same type of upbringing and opportunities as us.

One day, I caught Jeremiah staring at me. Suddenly, he laughed.

"You know what you are, girl?"

I shook my head.

"You're an apple," he held his hand in a fist in front of his mouth, faking coughing. "Red on the outside, white on the inside."

I know we are taught in our Native cultures to respect elders. But respecting them doesn't make them right.

While my academics improved, so did my mental, emotional, and spiritual health. I started speaking out about my experiences growing up with mental illness and addiction. I didn't take much time dwelling on where all of that originated; I was just so relieved to finally feel free of it.

Collegebound changed their name to Gateway to College, and they started getting national notoriety for their success in changing students' lives. When I graduated, they asked me to speak during classes with other Gateway youth, telling my story and inspiring hope. I loved speaking to other youth because their challenging questions, curiosity, and hope gave me so much good energy and inspiration, I came away with a feeling like being high. I was high on life, on the adrenaline of public speaking. Where I was once too shy and anxious to walk into a room full of students, I now felt powerful—I had something important to say, and people really wanted, even needed, to hear it.

From there, I started speaking at local, regional, and even national outlets related to Gateway to College. I've been on two national educational television shows. I've had people stop me on the street to tell me how inspiring my story is. I've had strangers ask to take photos with me.

As empowering as it was to participate in speaking engagements and TV shows, it was also very daunting. Everything always ended up alright, but leading up to every speaking engagement, I was completely panicked, in tears, on the verge of a meltdown. I knew I had to push through it, like I did every time before, but it took a lot out of me. I had to stop and take breaks, sometimes for even years at a time. Even writing about it now, it seems like a dream.

One of the funniest and strangest experiences happened to me during a TV show filming live in Washington, DC, when the TV host flubbed a question on camera directed towards me. The event was a very big deal. Gateway to College flew me (pregnant at twenty-eight) and a recent graduate to DC to be on a show for less than ten minutes. Prior to the show, we were each given a list of questions to prepare to answer on camera.

About a half hour before the show, we were brought into the hair and makeup trailer. There was a big protest in DC that day, and we ended up having to walk for miles in the August heat to the filming. I was two months pregnant, and I was pouring sweat by the time we got to the trailer. I was so anxious about my sweaty, pregnant body and my hair, which had poofed out in the humidity, that I could barely focus and kept feeling nauseous. I kept asking them to put more powder on my face while we waited, guzzling the free water. By the time we went on camera, I was in a full panic attack. The lights were bright as we sat on stage, and I couldn't get my breathing under control.

I was so focused on controlling my anxiety that I barely noticed when the host turned to me to ask a question, after briefly quizzing the other participant.

"And Leah, how about you? Who was the person who helped you when you started struggling in the program?"

I hesitated for several seconds, racking my brain for the correct answer, my mouth a wide O of surprise. He asked me the wrong question.

"Um . . ." I tried to figure out a way to address his slip up. He had directed the wrong question to me, one that was meant for the previous participant. "What?"

"Oh, um . . ." he looked down at his notes. "Somebody named Shawn?"

I looked up, searching the ceiling for the answer. "Who?"

"Oh! That wasn't you. That was *you*!" He laughed and turned back to the previous participant. I sat there in shock, thinking my ten seconds of fame was over.

He did come back to me, and I had the opportunity to tell my success story. I was calmer then, able to speak without shaking too much, thinking more clearly. The worst had already happened, so there wasn't much more to worry about.

Later, in our hotel room, my husband and I played the clip on repeat, laughing hysterically every time at my reaction.

Through all of those speaking engagements, the adrenaline and the anxiety and the empowerment, I never once thought about the origin of my depression and anxiety. The focus was centered completely on one question: "What was it about Gateway to College that turned my life around?"

Maybe that was the problem. We were asking the wrong question. I think the right question lies somewhere in: "What makes a person resilient?"

Hemblecha

I was about nineteen when my sweat lodge leader agreed to put me on the hill.

It was the third day of my hemblecha, and it was dusk, the time of day when the barrier between the spirit world and the real was the thinnest. I knew I had to move quickly in order to make it back to the safety of the circle that had been created to enclose my vision quest space.

My circle was filled with my biggest fear—spiders. I have something like arachnophobia; I get very tense and panicky when I see even one small spider, and when there are multiple spiders, my body fills with pure terror, and I freeze, unable to breathe. But by the third day of being surrounded by them, I almost welcomed their presence. I was so bored by then, and so hungry, that I welcomed any sort of distraction.

I had been warned in the sweat lodge before my vision quest: "If you have to leave the circle, do it quickly," Joe, the ceremony leader, had said. "As long as you stay in the circle, you will be safe." I grabbed the roll of toilet paper that had been left by my brothers and set two prayer sticks—sticks painted red with little pouches of tobacco, or prayer ties, tied to the ends—across a two-feet wide length of prayer ties, creating a doorway that allowed me to leave and return as necessary. The prayer ties were set in a circle and connected by red yarn around my star quilt, where I had spent the last three days fasting and praying.

Raising my hands to the skies, I spun clockwise and stepped outside. I leaned down to grab the prayer sticks and tucked them into the yarn belt tied around my waist. I tiptoed to a spot about ten yards away from the circle and squatted, keeping my head up and my senses aware—just in case. My legs shook, weak from the lack of sustenance; I hadn't consumed anything more the past three days than half a thermos of peppermint tea that Joe had brought me that morning. My stomach was so small by then that I couldn't finish the entire thermos and gave the rest to the altar and the spirits. I was surprised that I had to go at all.

Mid-squat, I thought I heard the brush moving on the other side of the circle. *It could be the wind.* There were so many small noises up on the hill, where I had thought it deafeningly quiet the first hours I sat there, consumed by the tranquility of the forest. That first night, I woke to the hissing of a cat I couldn't see. Startled, I was afraid to move—or breathe—and held myself tense, ready to run or fight, while I listened to its terrifying growl recede down the side of the hill into the darkness. I laid for hours afterward, listening to every *crunch* and *crackle* of sticks and leaves, until every pore of my skin seemed to respond to the sounds and movements around me. I had fallen asleep sometime the next morning, lulled by early birdcalls and the warmth of the rising sun.

If there is anything out there, I thought to soothe myself, *it is probably just another deer.*

There was a deer that woke me up on the second day of my hemblecha. I heard her snort and sat straight up; I didn't see her but heard her grunting and rushing off into the trees. I thought I saw a glimpse of her tan hoof slipping on the fallen branches that littered the ground, but it could have been a leaf. Before then, I didn't know that deer made noises like that.

She came back that night while I was sleeping. Again, I heard her deep snort right above my head. My eyes shot open and straight into hers; she was peering down into my face from above. She huffed and then backed away as I sat up slowly, hoping not to startle her. The moonlight shone on her fur, making it look like it was all in black and white, like an old movie, but still I could tell by the shades of shadow that she had beautiful tan, white, and black fur with a black tail. Her big, beautiful doe eyes reminded me of a starlet and reflected the moon, like camera lights in her pupils, and accentuated her ethereal beauty. Delighting in my admiration and awestruck expression, she twisted and turned her body this way and that, high-stepping like a pop star's backup dancer, her eyes trained on me, then dashed into the woods like a woodland sprite.

A few weeks prior, there was a peyote meeting in which all of my ceremony brothers and sisters and I had stayed up all night, praying and eating medicine. Long after most had gone to sleep, my brother Blaze and I found ourselves with the last bowl of mush (a mix of peyote tea and "mushed" buttons). Before he limped off to bed (our ceremony leader had a limp from a bad car accident many years before) Joe told us, "You can't go to sleep until it is all finished; it would be disrespectful to the medicine and the spirits."

So there we were, two Indians with one large bowl of mush meant for five. We split it in half and began eating. He couldn't finish, so I finished mine and his. By sunrise, I was floating sky high and in a completely different world. That's when Joe decided it was the right time to take me to Yoncalla to find my hemblecha spot—the spot where I would sit on the hill, fasting and praying for four days and four nights. Before we left, he brought out a bag of dried peyote and asked if I thought I could handle any more.

"Of course," I said, not wanting to seem weak or scared. He handed me the bag. I filled a plastic spoon with one large scoop and swallowed it whole. Blaze's eyes widened; I always felt like I had to prove myself in front of the ceremony men but would inevitably regret it later. The bitter, earthy, granular dried peyote was like dust or sand, coating the roof of my mouth and throat long after I swallowed. I breathed in, rolling my tongue around to get the rest mixed in with my saliva, tasting it all the way into my nose, and choked down the last particles, trying not to puke.

No wonder they call it medicine—even back then, nobody liked the taste.

As we headed down the highway in Joe's ocean-green Cadillac, I marveled at the immensity of the mountains against the clear blue skyline—as I watched them fly by, I could feel the earth inside them, the weight, the heaviness of years and life that they had seen. My perceptions became more and more expansive as the mescaline coursed through my body; I could hear the mountains singing. My ceremony brother, Diego, watched and laughed as my eyes bulged at passing trees and clouds. Anything manmade, I never saw on that trip; the concrete, the car, the buildings, they never registered. I wanted to fall into the earth and stay there until I disintegrated into it. I wanted to be more a part of it than I already was—I wanted to see from the top of the mountain and know what it felt like to stand as still as a tree for hundreds of years, listening to the wind and feeling the raindrops between my leafy fingertips.

When we got to the hill at Yoncalla, I took off into the forest.

"Diego," Joe pointed at me. "Go with her. Make sure she is okay."

Diego stayed right behind me, stepping exactly where I stepped. I turned around once we were in the dense forest.

"Where should I go?" I asked. He looked at me with wide eyes.

"Wherever you feel is right, mi-hija." I turned back around and began half-running, half-jogging up the hill, Diego struggling to keep up behind me.

"Wait up! You're going too fast." I could hear his breath lagging. I ran harder.

There was a tree branch in front of me; I ran underneath it. There was a puddle full of mud—I ran right through it, mud caking up to my knees. I paused, not knowing where to go next, breathing in the musky, sweet earth that smelled of recent rain and animal. A brilliantly bright orange butterfly brushed against my right arm and flew to my left. I began following it.

Diego was far behind me when I finally stopped. Looking around, I saw iktomi—spiders. Everywhere. There were spiders making gigantic webs in the trees, spiders in holes in the ground, spiderwebs floating in the air, the sunlight glinting off of their rainbow-colored threads that reminded me of flying carpets. As I stood with my mouth open in thrilled amazement, the silence overtook me, so peaceful. All of a sudden, I knew—this was where I was meant to sit, in this dangerous, wild, peaceful place.

Diego made his way slowly to the spot where I stood.

"This is it," I told him. "This is where I will pray."

The next day, after we got back to Portland and I had sobered up, the reality hit me. I had just chosen a spot filled with spiders, my biggest fear, probably many of them poisonous, some deadly. I cried in fear the day before my hemblecha. I thought about asking Joe if it was too late to change my mind, but I was too scared. I knew what he would say, and I didn't want to voice my fear to anyone, more afraid of the humiliation than my choice of site.

I prepared for my vision quest with the full expectation that I would probably die. There would be no one else on the hill with me. Joe would only come out once a day to check on me, and even then, we would barely speak. I could get bitten and die long before he checked on me the following day, not to mention the other bugs and animals in the forest in Yoncalla. Despite the fact that the risk of dying via spider bite was low, my fear wasn't rational. That's the thing about fear—it doesn't always make sense. It's not always linear. I don't know where my fear of spiders came from, but I know I have never felt pure dread like I do when confronted by a small body with eight legs. I figured if I prepared for the worst, anything better would be a saving grace.

However, once I was settled on the hill, the spiders kept me entertained. My fear slowly ebbed away as I watched a tiny baby jumping spider jump from one side of my star quilt to the other. It was so small, but if I concentrated long enough, I could see the outline of its eyes. It seemed to be watching me, just as I was watching it. I moved my finger close to its legs. It jumped to the left. I moved my finger close to its legs again. It jumped to the right. We went like this, back and forth, until I laughed so hard in delight that it jumped away into the brush. When I was really bored, having run out of things I could think of to pray about and songs that I could sing, I stared into the trees and waited until I could make out the multi-colored webs hanging above me and the strands of spiderwebs floating by in the wind. It kept my mind off of the hunger.

The ache in my stomach was the worst on the third day, when I got up to stretch and fell back down under my own weight. I had taken to doing yoga stretches throughout the day to keep my blood flowing, but started shaking so hard that I decided to stick with the ones I could do while sitting or lying down. Even then, my heart would beat so hard sometimes when I was just sitting that I would have to lay down and take deep breaths to calm myself. It was August in southern Oregon, so the heat also made it difficult to breathe and move around without feeling uncomfortable. It became more and more difficult to keep my thoughts straight. I concentrated really hard and prayed, reminding myself that I was sacrificing so that my hardest prayers, the ones about my fears and the illnesses and pains of my loved ones, would be answered. When I ran out of prayers again and my mind wandered, all I could think of was blueberry milkshakes and my stomach growled.

Creator, you better have something really good planned to keep me up here, I gazed into the sky, willing whatever higher power was listening to give me a sign that it wasn't all in vain. It had been a full day since the excitement of the deer. I had taken to memorizing constellations and astrological signs and all the Spanish words I knew and ordering them in my head to keep my mind off of food. I sucked on a rock to keep my saliva flowing and wished for a freak monsoon to pour down on me so that I could open my mouth accidentally and catch raindrops on my tongue.

Later, I thought to myself, *Be careful what you wish for.*

Hunching over and wiping myself, I looked down for just a moment and heard a *crunch*, loud and clear. A twig snapped. And then another.

I looked up and peered into the woods on the other side of the circle, squinting my eyes through the grayness of dusk. Had it gotten darker in just the mere moments I had been outside of the circle?

I slowly, quietly dug a hole and dropped the used paper into it as my heart fluttered. I dashed back to the circle and set down the prayer sticks as I heard another *snap*. My feet barely touched the ground as I spun with my hands in the air, hit the ground, and snatched up the sticks, closing the circle that was supposed to keep the spirit world out. My faltering faith slowly began to slip away as I frantically wracked my brain for reasons to believe in a God that wouldn't let me die that night, while the logical side of me screamed *RUN!*

Crouching low to the ground, I watched as black fur swayed back and forth above the bushes, coming slowly, lazily into view. I knew it was too late to run away. I searched around me for something to protect myself—if I had to, I could at least try to fight it. But there was nothing, besides Joe's ceremony pipe, lying in front of me on the altar.

I grabbed the pipe and held it in front of me, my right hand holding the stem, my left holding the bowl, closest to my heart. I needed all the protection I could get.

The bushes parted, and a nose peeked out, leading to a wide, tan face with jagged white-and-black markings that looked like lightning bolts. As he waddled toward me, his body came into view through the leaves. He was huge, even on all fours.

A black bear.

I didn't realize until later that I had been holding my breath the entire time. I kneeled with the pipe in my hands, facing the bear, with my body turned forward toward the setting sun and my waluta. He got to about five feet to my right before he stopped and sniffed the air, raising his head.

He looked right into my eyes. I didn't move. I didn't breathe. A shot of panic hit my chest and paralyzed me.

For about five seconds, we stared each other down. And then he turned around and ran into the woods, looking over his shoulder to see if I would follow. He disappeared into the trees. I prayed to Creator all night, thanking Him for keeping me alive and safe.

The last day, I rose with the sun and did my stretches with renewed strength. I knew I was in the home stretch. My body didn't shake or falter. I sang out my morning songs and finished my prayers.

I listened to the little boys at the camp yelling and laughing and yearned to be running and playing with them, so thankful to be living and young. Although I knew they were only a fifteen- or twenty-minute hike down the hill, they sounded so close I felt I could almost see them if I tried.

Joe came to get me with some ceremony helpers who took down my circle and wrapped it all in my star blanket. We left the altar for the spirits, with the offerings I had made prior to setting the site. I was not allowed to speak to my brothers or even look them in the eyes until after the closing sweat, where I offered my prayer ties to the fire and thanked everyone who had come with me to help me in my hemblecha.

"You look so skinny," said Ben when we were able to speak again. He handed me a banana while the rest finished cooking stew. I inhaled as I peeled the sweet fruit and smiled in relief as I bit into its creamy inside.

I will never forget the taste of that banana.

Fire Pin

In Girl Scouts the year I turned ten, I received a pin that celebrated my knowledge of fire. I had learned how to prepare a campfire shaped like a tipi and blasted flames and smoke out of the top, best suited for cooking marshmallows and hot dogs on camping trips. Although my family and friends were most impressed by this fire's gusto and strength, it did not last long and would burn quickly to ashes.

My favorite fire was the one that was much flatter to the ground and reminded me of my little brother's Lincoln Log set at home; logs were laid parallel to the ground, then more logs were set on top pointing the opposite way and lit via a small pile of twigs and moss underneath it. This was the fire that could keep a party going all night. My parents put me in charge of directing my younger brother and cousins in fire-making activities whenever we camped out at the Oregon beach or up in the woods of Washington during family gatherings. This fire wasn't as cool-looking as the other one because it wasn't as big and didn't look like a volcano erupting when lit—but once it got going, it kept everyone warm all night and lasted until the morning.

In Girl Scouts, I learned that the tips of Ready-Strike matches, when dipped in my mom's favorite red rose nail polish, were then rendered waterproof; I "borrowed" an empty film canister from my dad to keep them in. (I later discovered that he used these canisters for stashing pot because you couldn't smell it through the thick plastic.) I punched two holes in the sides near the top and pulled a piece of red yarn through to make a necklace and wore it all summer, along with my newly earned fire pin.

With the pin came a certain amount of responsibility; I knew to clear a large enough area around the fire and line it with large river rocks so any sparks that flew outside the circle would dissipate by the time they landed. Because my mother trusted me with my fires, she allowed me to create a small fire pit of my own in the front yard that I would sit at for hours on end, making little fires and staring into the flames before putting them out with dirt and water. Fire entranced me and made me feel calm.

That summer, when I would stare into the little flames, I thought about my birth brother. No one ever told me that I had one; I don't think they knew for sure anyway. But something inside me told me that I had another brother who needed me, too. I don't know how I knew, but gazing into that fire, I felt as if it opened a portal inside me, one that connected me to the sibling I knew was out there somewhere.

The need in me to find my birth brother, my whole birth family, grew over the years until it became a huge rock of depression and anger and confusion that threatened to chase me down and flatten me every chance it got. I felt like my past was a puzzle that I was only given a few of the pieces to; I was the picture, incomplete, without those missing pieces. When I turned sixteen, my parents hired a lawyer to get my adoption records from the local courthouse. Because it was a closed adoption, the records he found were redacted so that identifying details about my birth parents were blacked out; however, they missed a mention of my grandfather's name—Reza Beyk. From that name, I was able to find the names of my birth mother and birth father: June Beyk and Edwin Francis Blackfeather. From the adoption records, I knew that Edwin—Eddie—was an enrolled tribal member. June was half-Persian. There was very little that I knew about either of them from those papers, but it was all I had to start with.

When I turned twenty-one, I decided to transfer from my community college in the Pacific Northwest to a school in tiny Spearfish, South Dakota—Black Hills State University—to look for my birth family. I chose Black Hills State because it was the closest college to the reservation. The reservation had a college, but no housing, and I didn't know anyone there. I liked my new school because I could major in journalism and minor in the Lakota language.

The first thing I did once I got acquainted with the town and the school was to call the tribal registry in Pine Ridge, two hours southeast of Spearfish. A woman there named Harriet told me that she couldn't release any information about my lost relatives, even if she had it. However, she could contact anyone that she could find on file and give them my information—it was up to them to contact me from there.

It was 5:35 p.m. when my cell phone rang—eleven minutes after I spoke to Harriet. I was getting ready for my class on media and journalism and let it ring a few times while I finished placing my books in my bag and zipped up my winter coat over layers of clothes. The room where the class was held was freezing, even on hot days, but it was October and the temperature in the Black Hills in the fall was either cold enough to snow or hot enough to wear shorts, never in-between.

That day was the first we had frost—I had never felt my nose hairs freeze up before and always thought that I had boogers hanging out my nose until I mentioned it to a friend one day. She laughed and said, "Welcome to the Midwest! That's just the dry air here. I don't even notice it anymore." I never got used to the feeling and compulsively checked my nostrils in the bathroom mirror before class to make sure there was nothing there.

"Hello?" I answered as I raced around the room looking for my apartment keys.

The responding voice came in the tone of a take-charge kind of woman. Her voice was rushed, blunt, direct, like a butcher knife chopping onions.

"This is Levi's mom."

"Who?"

"Levi's mother. Do you know what I am talking about?" She seemed agitated that I didn't.

"No . . . I mean, I think I do . . ." I guessed, ". . . are you talking about my birth brother?"

"I think so. Who was your mom?"

"June Beyk. She's Iranian-Persian. But my birth dad is Eddie Blackfeather . . . Edwin. He's the one I'm looking for . . . I mean, I'm looking for both." Words seemed to trip off my tongue, my brain trying to process how quickly things were starting to happen. "But . . . he has the information I need and family history to get enrolled in my tribe." I was shaking, but feeling more assured that she wouldn't hang up if I didn't respond quickly.

"Yeah, that's him, your dad," I sensed a smile, or a curse—maybe both. "He took off a long time ago, just after you all were born. There was another little girl, you know. There were two of you."

I could picture two dark-skinned little girls with long hair in braids and pink dresses. Then I remembered we would have been much younger, just babies.

"Yeah, my adoptive mom guessed that there were probably a few of us. The adoption papers indicate that he might've had a couple different marriages."

"Yep, that sure sounds like Eddie," She laughs. "How old are you?"

"Twenty-one."

"Levi will be twenty on Christmas Eve. He's our holiday baby." Her voice is suddenly warmer, gentler, slower. "Oh, I'm Wanda, by the way. You can call me anytime you want, but we are going to leave it up to Levi if he wants to call you. He knows . . . he's always known about the adoption. We'll see him again this weekend, and then we'll tell him. I'd rather do it in person than over the phone, you know?"

"Yes, of course." There was a pause. It was beginning to sink in that I didn't know this woman I was sharing such a personal moment with. It all seemed so terribly unreal to me. I had been waiting so long for something to happen since the day my plane touched down in Rapid City in August, before school; yet, when it started happening, it seemed too much, too fast.

"Hey," she said. "Are you okay?"

"Yeah . . . yeah, I'm alright," I lied.

"Good. Do you have some kind of spiritual support out here?"

"Well," I attempted to gather my thoughts. "I just moved to Spearfish. This is why I came, to find . . . I gave some tobacco to a lady out here. She's an instructor at the school. She's a sun dancer. I asked her to help me find a sweat lodge."

"Well, be careful," she warned, "of who you get involved with out here, okay?"

"Okay."

Another pause. We both held our breath. When she spoke next, it was very quiet, very unlike the voice that was speaking before.

"You know, you gotta be strong now. People never turn out to be how you expect them to be out here. Everyone's really . . . poor. I bet you grew up in a middle-class family, huh?" She wasn't wrong. "What do your parents do?"

"My mom's a nurse, and my dad is a warehouse supervisor."

"Well, yeah . . . then things are definitely going to be real different out here for you. Are you ready?"

I laughed. The laughter broke against the walls of my chest. Wanda was silent.

"Probably not," I admitted.

When I hung up the phone, I sat, stunned, watching the second hand on the clock gently push the minute hand closer to the time when class would start, and then farther. I couldn't think, I couldn't breathe. If I could think, I wouldn't know where to begin. The floor beneath me suddenly seemed as if it were on top of my head and slanted sideways, falling off into space, and with it, everything I knew to be true about my life.

I felt the rush of tears coming up like after a night of Jack Daniels and dancing, when everything around me would be spinning; and crying, like throwing up, was a release. It was like trying to breathe underwater. I came out the other end of my pool of grief feeling fresh, yet still very raw. I clenched my fists around my elbows and across my stomach as I headed late to class, barely remembering to breathe and to look both ways at the crosswalk. I forgot my book bag and didn't care; the academic value of the class meant nothing to me just then. I just didn't want to be alone with what I was feeling.

The class was a long one, so it was dark when I got back to my on-campus apartment. My phone, still on silent, buzzed in my pocket, against my hip. I got that feeling you get right as you crest the height of a roller coaster, right before the drop, adrenaline and fear and giddiness at once, taking your breath away.

"Hi, Leah?" His voice was deep, unsure. "This is your brother, Levi."

He said he lived in Rapid City, only forty-five minutes away.

"Can I come see you? Like, right now?"

I answered, "Yes, come now!" It was like he was walking out of an impossible dream.

When I opened the door to his knock, I didn't know what to expect. His skin surprised me; he was much lighter than I was. He was six foot one, tall and lean, with an ironic grin. When we hugged, he felt strong, despite how skinny he looked. We took a picture on my camera phone right away to send to our friends and family, asking whether or not people thought we looked alike. Everyone said yes; we had the same eyes and the same mischievous grin on thin lips, always ready to crack a sarcastic retort. We had the same high Indian cheekbones, and the distinguished Persian nose that always made me feel like I wasn't nearly as pretty as the blonde-haired, blue-eyed girls in school who had cute little pug noses, or the ones who were tall and brunette and slender, whose noses were straight and intelligent-looking. Levi and I had noses with character; for the first time, I didn't feel alone.

Later on, we would discover that there were other things we had in common, such as our long intuitive fingers, our graceful hands, our skinny toes. We could volley jokes back and forth for hours, chasing wits in circles until something else came along to distract us. We could both be playful and silly, or silent and moody.

He couldn't stay long, but he promised to come again soon.

Four days after we first met, he came to visit again. We looked up our birth mom's father on the internet. We hadn't found a number for June, but they did have a listing for a Reza Beyk in Littleton, Colorado. I made Levi call him and sat still as a deadly silent winter night, when no one ventures out in the cold and the snow blankets all sound.

"Hello? Is this Reza?" he asked, looking upward and to the right, at the ceiling as he talked. "I think you're my grandpa."

Levi put us on speakerphone so we could both listen. Reza had a thick accent, stressing unexpected syllables. He was warm, but brief.

"Yes," he said, which sounded like "*yes-ah.*" "We live in Littleton, Colorado. It is near Denver, you know Denver?" His accent reminded me of Jafar from *Aladdin*. "Your mother is June. She lives in Longmont, on the other side of Denver from us. That is where your siblings grew up."

"You will come see us sometime?" he asked. "Yes, you will come see us," he answered.

He gave us the numbers for our Persian aunts, our older brother and sister in Denver and Loveland, and June.

Reza, who we later learned preferred to be called "Granddad," called June and told her to call us. When the phone rang, I nearly jumped out of my seat.

"Hello? Leah?" Her voice was deep for a woman, thick and slow, syrupy. "This is June. Your mom. Your birth mom." I held my breath, my chest tight.

"Hi," I breathed out, sounding so young, even to myself. "Levi is here, too."

"Levi?" she asked. "Oh, yes, Levi. I named him Levi from the Bible. Sid's name is short for Obsidian. Did you know you have siblings? Sid and Petra. Here, Sid is here. Let me put him on the phone."

"Hello, Leah?" His voice was deep like molasses. I felt instantly safe, listening to him talk.

"Did you know that when you apply heat and pressure to specific kinds of rocks, they can actually turn into gold?" I didn't know that. He told me, "I got a blowtorch." And "I would never have let anything bad happen to you, ever, if we had been raised together."

We talked until four a.m., when we both fell asleep listening to each other breathing. Levi had left hours earlier. I woke up later, mid-afternoon, my ear burning from lying on the phone. My phone had died while I was sleeping.

When I was a teenager, I started going to sweat lodges. I found a group of spiritual people I felt comfortable with, and they taught me how to be a fire keeper for our lodge. I learned that keeping fire meant spending the day with the fire, from early in the morning, hours before the ceremony, until long after the ceremony was completed. I learned how to build a fire like my long-burning fire, but bigger and built around large river rocks. When the rocks were burning red hot, that's when the sweat could commence.

I learned how to pray while gathering and splitting the wood, building the fire, lighting it, and keeping it burning. I burnt my fingers and my nails and my feet and my legs. I've lost sections of my hair to it, and one time, a full eyebrow. I learned not to be afraid of fire, but to respect it. It's cleansed away my grief, kept me alive, and taught me lessons. It is hypnotizing, healing.

Fire is important in my family. We build fires to gather around during the summer, winter, fall, spring. In every type of weather, we've gathered around a fire to keep warm, drink, share stories, laugh. Fire brings people together, brings families together. I believe it brought my birth family together, from the very day I received that Girl Scouts fire pin, when that niggling feeling in my chest told me that I had a birth brother and that I needed to find him.

Cekpa

"Mom, what was she like? Did you ever meet her? Why did she give me up?" I imagine my little olive-skinned face, long Persian nose already starting to show its shape, eyes a shade my mother called dark chocolate.

"Well," she said, smoothing her napkin as she finished chewing. We ate lots of peanut butter and jelly sandwiches when I was growing up. She likes hers with butter.

I imagine us sitting at the small wooden dining room table we had in the little house where I grew up. It was small, but perfect for our little family. Despite the lack of room, my parents managed to squeeze a piano in the corner, gifted to my mother from her own grandmother. She hoped I would become a pianist.

"Your birth mother is Persian, and we have reason to believe her family is very wealthy," she would say, bending down so we could talk, face to face. My adoptive mother's skin was not much lighter than my own, but her nose was straighter, her hair lighter, her eyes more rounded, a spattering of dark brown sun spots flung across her face like a Picasso painting. "But your birth father is Native American and poor, so it was never going to work out from the beginning."

She did remember something about my birth mother's family moving to the States when the Shah of Iran was overthrown. She inferred that my birth mother's father was somehow connected to the Shah and that the family had to leave Iran for their own safety because of their affiliation with him.

"Maybe you are a Persian princess!" she exclaimed, eyes and mouth wide open at the thought. She loved to speculate about my heritage with me.

We made up stories about why my Persian birth mother had to give me up.

"Maybe your birth mother is a Persian princess and her family threatened to disown her for marrying a poor Indian boy," she would say. "Some women in countries like Iran are stoned to death for less. Maybe she had no choice."

"But whatever her reason was, sweetie, I know it had to be something really big to have to give you up. I know she loved you."

That's the story I told people when they asked about my adoption, long into early adulthood. I could have been a Persian princess.

Then, I met June.

A week after Levi and I called June the first time, Levi invited me to come stay with him in Rapid City. He wanted to throw me a "homecoming party" and introduce me to his friends, his girlfriend, his girlfriend's family, and his son, Aiden, who was two.

He came and picked me up and brought me back to Rapid. On the way, we called June and told her we were together, and that Levi was throwing me a homecoming party. We were laughing and giggling; I suppose she felt left out.

Levi lived with his girlfriend, Tianna; Tianna's mom, Stacy; Tianna's sister, Catie; and Aiden. Levi and Tianna had lost their second child only months before—a little boy, Dayton—from sudden infant death syndrome. The six of them inhabited a small, messy, two-bedroom trailer in a trailer park on the west side of Rapid Shitty. Stacy had a little dog that shat on the enclosed porch outside, so when you walked in, you had to walk over piss and shit to get to the door. Just hold your breath.

Poor Stacy had a lot on her hands. She still had her grown daughters living with her, plus her daughter's boyfriend and son. She had no desire to clean up after them all and spent most days hiding out in her room with her thriller books and real-life mystery shows and her cigarettes. To get to her room, you had to hop over a hole in the floor.

The trailer was filled with all kinds of smoke. Cigarette smoke, pot smoke, bacon grease smoke, smoke from our Totino's pizzas burning in the oven. The kids ran that house, and ran wild.

When I got there, there were already other twenty-somethings filling the house with music, booze, pot, and their bodies, their smells competing with the smells already lingering in that trailer. They were watching some disgusting Japanese horror film—a scene in which a woman is torturing a princess because she is jealous, pushing slivers of wood under the princess' fingernails, into her skin, to make her scream. Bass pumping from the kitchen, all the lights turned low.

"Leah, I want you to meet my brother," said Levi. "Not like my birth brother, like us, but I grew up with him. This is Kenny." A tall Native guy with spiky hair and a pockmarked face shook my hand, pursing his lips and lifting his chin at me, almost like blowing a kiss, but harder, rougher. I smiled and squeezed his hand flirtatiously.

It was in that environment that we got a call from June. I stepped outside to answer it, Levi trailing behind me. I walked out into the tiny yard, away from the dog shit smell and noise. I was three whiskey shots in and maybe a Jell-O shot or two, also. (Broke rez kids can't afford chasers, so we just drank it straight.)

"Hello?" I answered. "June?"

"Leah, I'm on my way, okay?"

"Wait, what?" I replied after a moment of liquor-fueled hesitation. "Where? Here? Rapid?"

"Yeah," she said, decidedly. "I'm coming to get you."

When I got off the phone, I turned to Levi, jumping up and down. It had started to snow, light flakes catching on my eyelids and dancing in the streetlights.

"She's coming here, right now! She's coming to get us and take us to Denver to meet our family."

Levi and I headed inside, where he yelled out that everyone had to leave, immediately. We had to start getting ready. It didn't matter that she was five hours away still or that we didn't have anything to do to get ready besides take showers and naps. We just needed to feel like we were preparing.

My phone woke me later, in the middle of the night, with a buzz. I had fallen asleep on Levi's couch.

"Levi," I called out in a hushed whisper at the door to Tianna's room. "She's here." He dragged himself out of bed, grabbed his bag, and followed me out the door.

It was still snowing, now fat, heavy flakes that stuck to my eyelashes and made them blurry. I saw a light-colored car in the driveway, the headlights on, further blinding me. The snow was falling so thick I didn't even see her get out of the car.

She was short, medium-to-dark skinned with dark features. Her hair was short and thick, cut just below her chin. She walked right up and stared into my eyes, smiling, and then she hugged me tight, for a long time.

"You are so beautiful!" she exclaimed, as she let go. "And you, Levi, you're so handsome!" She hugged him, too. I was speechless. She pulled back and stared at us both like we were the most beautiful, magical things she had ever seen. She seemed in awe of us, nothing, nobody Native kids. From the very moment she laid eyes on us, I knew we were important to her.

"Well, come on, let's get out of the snow. You've got your bags?"

When are we coming back? I wondered.

The first time I spoke to June, that night on the phone with Levi, June told me their story. It wasn't far from the story my adoptive mother told me growing up. She was raised in Iran with her family—my granddad, grandmother, her older brother Bijan, and her two sisters, Shirin (older) and Jila (younger)—until she was fourteen. My grandmother was from Oklahoma, and she and my grandfather met when he was in America doing business. He brought her to Iran to start a family, but she never felt comfortable there, and when the Shah was overthrown, it was too dangerous for them to stay. They spent some time in Europe on their way back to the States, and then eventually landed in a suburb outside of Denver.

The first time I saw Granddad's house, I was in awe. It was a McMansion, in the middle of a development of other McMansions.

From the outside, it looked the same as all the others, painted in various shades of brown and beige, with an impressive entryway framed by a high arched overhang. Huge palm-style plants on the porch, fancy cars parked in front of the garage like all the other garages, professionally managed HOA-grade lawn. (I know about this lifestyle now, but at age twenty-one, I just knew they were richer than me.)

Inside, it was exotic and immaculate. It felt like walking into another country. The houseplants were bigger than me, towering over my head. Persian rugs covered everything—the floors, the walls, even the tables. Huge, engraved silver platters hung in the middle of the biggest walls. Intricate silver tea systems adorned dust-free, dark wood furniture. Nothing was out of place—no books or mail scattered on surfaces, no shoes on the white carpet, no cups or plates left out to be put away later, no clutter. It was like someone came in daily and cleaned up after them. The floors looked freshly swept, vacuumed, mopped.

"Come in, come in!" My grandfather met June, Sid, and me at the door. He was tiny, shorter than me, and frail—yet his smile and positive energy belied his body and immediately lifted my spirits.

"Leah!" He clasped my right hand with both of his, gently, his palms dry and warm. He looked into my eyes, searching. His skin looked like worn, crumpled paper—and a similar shade of gray. "I am so glad you are here. Welcome!" I was starting to get used to being stared at for uncomfortable periods of time by my birth family, their eyes roaming my face, drinking me in.

"Here, take off your shoes." The first rule I learned—no shoes in Granddad's house.

I slipped off my dirty, cheap five-dollar Old Navy flip flops.

"You have no socks!" he cried in astonishment. Concerned, he asked, "Are your feet cold? You need socks."

"I'm okay, Granddad!" I laughed. "Don't worry about it. I'll be fine."

"No, no, no . . . you need socks. Do you want me to find you some socks?" He stared down at my feet.

June laughed, watching the interaction. "Leah, you should just let him get you some socks."

"No, it's okay!" I repeated.

"Are you sure? It's cold in here. We have air conditioning."

"He won't stop," June whispered to me, her arms crossed, hip jutting out.

"I'm fine! I promise. I'll be fine." I was surprised at the intensity of his concern.

"Okay. Alright." His shoulders slumped in defeat. "If you are sure."

Later, June explained this particular aspect of Persian culture to me, as we sat on the deck in barely used wicker patio furniture, staring out at the setting sun in the endless Colorado sky, drinking red wine much too fancy for me to appreciate. She stared into the distance, black sunglasses covering her eyes, her shoulder-length, thick, salt-and-pepper hair blowing messily in the breeze. She kept patting it back in place as she talked.

"It's a custom to offer something three times. And you're supposed to refuse at least twice, and then, if you accept on the third time, that means you really mean yes. But if they don't offer a third time, then it means that it's not sincere. The third time is when you know if they really mean it, and then it's okay for you to accept.

"It comes from people being really poor. Like, if we lived in Iran, and if you came to my house, it would be rude if I didn't offer you tea. But maybe I can't afford tea, or we don't have much left . . . so then, I would only offer twice. Or maybe I just don't really want you to stay too long!" She laughed, thinking about it. "But if I have plenty, and I really want you to stay and talk with me, I would ask you three times."

A pause.

"But then, if you refused the third time, that would be rude of you."

Another pause as we took in the view, thinking. The wind was chilly, but it was worth the scenery.

"Persian people are very courteous and accommodating. They are very social. It isn't like here, where everyone is doing their own thing, even in their own houses. People like to get together, to talk, to have tea; especially in the evenings. Being a good host is very important."

✦

Granddad takes being a good host very seriously. He is a fabulous cook. Every time I visited Granddad's house with June or my birth siblings, we vowed to try to finish all the food.

"Oh my god!" we'd exclaim. "I miss homecooked Persian food so much!" I didn't grow up with access to Persian culture in my adoptive family, so my only experience of Persian food was Granddad's.

Me: "I hope he makes chicken jujube."

Sid: "I hope he makes that beef stew dish, what's it called?"

June: "I have to ask him if he knows how to make tadig. I can never make it right, with the crust, without burning it."

We'd walk from the bus to the Persian Hilton, as we called it. Sometimes in the snow or the sweltering heat. Granddad met us at the door, open arms, same warm smile, hugs.

Grandmother Eleanor would hug us from her bed when she woke from her nap. She was always sick, an ache in her bones that nothing eased. Occasionally, if she was feeling well enough, she'd come sit with us for a while. While her body was frail, her spirit was always so strong. Not one for small talk, she wanted to talk about deep things with the small bit of time she had with us.

Grandmother moved slowly, with her little metal and plastic cane, the tap tap tapping through the hallway announcing her entrance long before you'd actually see her. As small as Granddad was in frame, she was smaller, much more stooped. Her wrinkled skin was albino white, and she had a puff of platinum, cotton-candy-spun hair like a halo around her head.

She moved slowly from the arthritis and polymyalgia and laid in bed most of her days. They have a winter home in Arizona where the dry heat eases her throbbing bones.

Shortly after I met her, I was playing soccer in a pick-up game at school; I was the only girl among a group of Asian and Arab boys. I played rough, like the guys, rougher than them even because they were afraid to be too rough with a girl. Most of them were especially gentle until I pushed them too far. Two of them teamed up and side-tackled me, their legs tangling my ankles, weaving in and out between my feet. Something popped, and my ankle turned sunset colors, swollen like a grapefruit. I remember that one of the boys, smaller than me, felt terrible and carried me off the field and all the way to the school clinic on his back. I was on crutches for a month, hopping my way up the three floors of my elevator-free campus apartment that had been built in the '20s.

When I fell, I instinctively put my hands out to catch me. Less than a year later, I was diagnosed with severe tendonitis. Fifteen years later, I have carpal tunnel. I know when it's going to rain, and I can tell how much by how painful my hands feel. As a writer, both for my day job and as my passion, my fingers constantly ache, and I use CBD lotion when I bead to take the edge off.

I always wonder how long it's going to take before I'm like Grandmother.

For all her aches and pains, her blue eyes are bright, quick, intelligent. She's always aware of what is going on around her, always reading people. But she's not soft. She is direct, with a midwestern charm and an Oklahoman accent, even after all these years. When I first met her, she told me about growing up on her family's farm.

"There wasn't anything to do out there," she laughed. "I wanted to travel."

While my time with her has always been in short spurts, she still sends me cards on my birthday and Christmas, and she follows my Facebook posts, "liking" photos of our family. Sometimes she comments or sends me short messages, telling me she loves me.

I keep writing around June. I sit down to write about her, and I swirl around the perimeter, writing about everyone closer to her, but not her. Maybe there is a part of me still processing, maybe there is a lot I stuff down, not ready yet to sift through.

June and my sister Petra are both shorter than me. Petra hates that her little sister is taller than her. (Here I go writing about someone else again. I touch on June, and then step back.)

When I think about June, I start with her hair, something I obviously inherited from her. When I was little, and even still, people liken my hair to horsehair. It is coarse and thick, not just in the amount of individual hairs on my head but in the thickness of each actual hair. When I rub my hair together next to my ear, it sounds like paper crinkling.

When I met June, I was only twenty-one. I cut my hair in a short bob cut before I moved to South Dakota to find my birth family, and I had blond streaks in it. June wore her hair shoulder-length in a blunt cut. It made her head look bigger, with how thick her hair was, emphasizing the thickness, yet her face seemed to get lost in the forest. Petra's hair is the same. She buzzcuts half her head in the summer in an undercut, and it's still thick with only half of it left. (There I go again.) June wasn't dyeing her hair then, so it was peppered with gray, making her skin look darker.

June has an amazing smile, but she was very serious at the time I met her. She was experimenting with her medication a lot, taking different dosages, not taking them altogether, trying different medications, throwing them all away and starting over again. When she was well, she called and texted me a lot wanting to talk, asking me how school was going, when I was coming out again to visit. I knew when she was off her medication because I wouldn't hear from her for weeks, sometimes months.

Her eyes are like her mother's, bright and watchful. June is a watcher, very much an empath. If I am sad, I can glance at her, and she will be crying, tears pooling at the corners of her eyes.

Her nose is like mine, very Persian, long with a little hook at the tip. But I also have my dad's nose—like those pictures of Plains chiefs in headdresses. The little racist white kids at my church growing up called me a witch. I always wished I had a cute tiny button nose like my adoptive brother, who always seemed to fit in even though he was darker than me.

June is olive-complexioned, but my siblings and I are a light brown. Our dad was darker. Petra, Sid, and I are about the same tone, while Levi is gray. There is no better way to describe him. His hair, skin, and eyes have a grayish tint. Our birth family on the rez swears he came out red. June doesn't remember Levi being red, but she also cannot remember which hospital, or even which town, we were in when I was born.

When she and her sisters were teenagers, June and her older sister Shirin ran away from home and joined a cult. They were drugged and things happened to them, things June can't, or won't, remember.

On the few occasions I tried to broach the subject, wanting to know what happened to her to trigger her psychosis, June would shut down. Her eyes went somewhere far away, and she stopped talking. I hate making her feel that way, so I gave up trying to dig for information long ago. All I know is that something bad, maybe many bad things, happened.

She and Shirin were brainwashed and had to be "deprogrammed." They joined a Christian church to get well, and that's where June met my father, Eddie.

Edwin Francis Blackfeather. June's version of Eddie is that he was very charming but dangerous, like something glittery and shiny and sharp, sharp enough to cut. Their relationship was tumultuous. He abused her. She'd kick him out, they would make up, and then, for a time, things would be okay again. He was an alcoholic; he was after her family's money.

When she got pregnant with Petra, Granddad offered him a truck and a thousand dollars to leave her. Eddie was proud he didn't accept. But he abused her more. She kicked him out, then let him come back, and they had Sid. This went on four times. Petra, Sid, and I are each about a year apart, and then Levi was born a year and a half after me. So for almost five years, she was constantly pregnant and taking care of babies and/or toddlers, sometimes on her own, when Eddie was gone on a binge. And through all of this, abuse.

It is no wonder she had a break from reality between Sid and me. She was pregnant with me when she went into psychosis. There is research that extreme stress can affect a baby in the womb. There is also research that schizophrenia can be triggered by extreme stress.

She couldn't keep me after that; she was in no shape to keep me. She couldn't even hold me before she gave me up.

You, Aurora, first met your grandma JuJu when you were three and Acacia was just a baby. It was the summer after Acacia was born, and we were in the middle of selling our house. I was thirty-four; I had you at age thirty-one, and I had Acacia when I was thirty-three. When we had the house up for sale, we moved in with Grandma Schröder and lived in the ADU at the back of her house. It was easier to show the house when we weren't living in it.

It was a nice set-up. We had our own little one-bedroom apartment to ourselves, with a bathroom and kitchen and small living room. There was a long hallway, too, where you played, bouncing a ball, or racing a truck, or just running in your own little space, back and forth.

We were cramped, but it wasn't terrible. I slept on the couch in the living room sometimes when Cacia woke up in the middle of the night, wanting to nurse and then roll around and play. You slept in a little toddler bed in our bedroom with your daddy. You had night terrors sometimes, so your daddy would put you to bed while I managed Acacia in the other room.

It was small, but you loved seeing your Grandma Schröder and aunties every day. We'd have dinner with them most nights, us ladies drinking wine and playing with you girls.

Grandma Schröder had a pool in the backyard, twenty feet away from our French doors. We opened those doors from the living room and played in the water all day during the summer. In the mornings, when it was cooler, we'd let you explore the backyard on your own for hours. She had a huge yard with a locked gate, and the pool was fenced, so you were safe out there. I kept the door cracked and checked on you frequently. There was a horseshoe pit at the end of the property, and you loved to play in the sand.

After we accepted the offer on the house, we had two months before the new owners moved in, so Grandma JuJu came and stayed down at our old house at night and played with you girls during the day. She was a little strict with you, like her parents were when she was little, and you didn't like that much. But she read you books and played with you, and she rocked Cacia for hours so I could have a break.

I remember she and Grandma Schröder sat and talked all night the night before she left, drinking wine and speaking softly, spatters of laughter reaching our apartment rooms while I put you to sleep. So many times while we lived there, Grandma Schröder rocked Acacia to sleep while I read you books and sang you lullabies and patted your back. While you quit nursing a year earlier than your little sister, you slept with your Binky until you were almost four. We were worried it might ruin your teeth, so we made you give it up while we lived there. Your daddy kept that Binky for years after.

I came out and got Acacia, gently lifting her off Grandma Schröder's chest and carrying her to the apartment. I took a shower and got ready for bed, and then fell asleep nursing Acacia.

Later that night, I woke to the sound of laughter. I peeked through the windows on our door leading to the main house and saw Grandma Schröder and Grandma JuJu still chatting, a small lamp on. *What a lovely world that my birth mother and my adoptive grandmother can laugh and drink wine late into the night,* I thought.

I was so nervous about that first visit, just because I was a new mom and hadn't really hosted anyone before with a baby and toddler to manage. But I remember it being a very emotional visit, and we were all sad when she left.

We saw Grandma JuJu one more time after that, right before the COVID-19 pandemic hit, when I was thirty-four and you were four, Aurora. Acacia was only a year old. It was your first time on an airplane. (It is amazing that, at five, you still remember. We are now in the middle of the pandemic, and you keep begging me to take you on a plane. You girls are too young to get vaccinated, so we have to keep you quarantined; a trip is out of the question.) I was terrified of taking a toddler and a baby on an airplane, but you both just slept the whole time, except when Cacia nursed.

There was a snowstorm in Denver. It was Thanksgiving weekend, and we flew your cousin Lacee, Levi's daughter, from Rapid to meet us for the holiday. Petra was in prison, and Sid was living on the streets, so you three girls had your JuJu to yourselves.

We stayed at Granddad's, and he and Grandmother were so thrilled to meet you. Granddad teased you, Aurora, and you yelled at him. It was adorable—you were so tiny, and so angry, stamping your little feet at the top of the stairs; you were angrier when we laughed, not able to help ourselves.

Granddad and JuJu took us to the mall. Malls in Denver are not like malls in Portland. Malls in Denver are like going to an indoor amusement park. We played games, rode an indoor train, saw elves, and played in bouncy houses and indoor parks. We ate ice cream that was flattened and rolled into flowers, sprinkled with candy. You begged Granddad to buy you pink ice cream, and then you took a few bites and ran off, giggling.

We rode ponies and dragons throughout the mall, Cacia sleeping in a carrier on my chest and you riding with your daddy. You wouldn't let him drive . . . he kept trying to teach you how, and you ran into people and kiosks, and we got in trouble and had to take the little creatures back.

You adored your older cousin Lacee, who was twelve at the time. She is sassy and smart and funny, and she doted on both you girls. She took you on rides and let you tag along everywhere she went. She carried Acacia for me and helped entertain you while I nursed. On Black Friday, JuJu took us to Target to take advantage of all the deals, and I splurged on gifts for Lacee as a thank you.

I'm so glad Granddad and Grandmother got to meet you. Who knows when we will be able to see them next, and they are getting older and more frail. It may be that, when we are able to travel again, it might be too late.

Little Girl With a Hole in Her Chest

My birth mother does not remember where I was born.

She knows it was in Colorado, somewhere in the Denver area. She doesn't remember what time. She doesn't remember much about the labor. She doesn't remember who was there, or if it was difficult or easy, or what the nurses or doctor said to her. Not the way she felt, or how long it took or if she even saw my face. Not if she screamed or if I screamed or even if she had a vaginal birth or cesarean. She doesn't remember how long she was in the hospital or if anyone was there with her. There is a hole in her mind where her memory should be.

What June remembers is that she danced in a rainstorm with my sister Petra when she was eight months pregnant with me. She gave me a secret name—Raindance—because she knew she would never dance with me. She remembers that they named me Baby Blackfeather on my birth certificate because I was going to be adopted out. She remembers telling them she didn't want to hold me because she didn't know if she would be able to give me back.

June remembers my siblings' births—even Levi's, and he was adopted out, just like me. She remembers to tell her family about Levi. She forgets to tell them about me, stuffing me down and out of her mind, someplace where her trauma and pain reside. I am synonymous with her pain.

I am a little girl walking around with a hole in my chest where my cekpa would be. Your cekpa is connected to the land you came from. I don't know where I came from. I am from nowhere and everywhere. I am every little girl walking around with a hole in her chest where her heart should be.

Seven Phases

in pictures of me and my sister
i forget where she ends and i begin, like twins
we mistake ourselves for each other.
in her presence, i either lose autonomy or take comfort in the fact
that there's someone out there just like me, oglala and persian, all mixed up
in one nose
another girl who hears more than the beat of one drum, more than one voice.

I wake up to the sweetest little giggle, like bells tinkling.

A tiny face peeks out at me from behind a hallway wall in my birth mother's home, a house I do not, at first, recognize, as I blink my bleary eyes.

The face disappears again. The tinkling giggle does not.

I sit up on the gray, broken-in couch, looking around at the white, sparse walls and arched doorways. There is one large painting done in pastel watercolors, muted but colorful tones, on the wall directly across from me. It's a woman dancing, but there is something almost tragic about her dance, pensive. June painted it. Art runs in our blood.

The little cherub prances out from behind the doorway again, her straw-colored hair a wild puff of cotton candy crowning her forehead, her pink cheeks flushed against light skin. She's so different from me. I wonder what her mother looks like.

According to Wikipedia, methamphetamine is a stimulant drug that affects the central nervous system. It was discovered in 1893 and exists as levomethamphetamine and dextromethamphetamine (dextromethamphetamine is stronger; levomethamphetamine is available over-the-counter as an inhaled nasal decongestant). Methamphetamine is also used as a second-line treatment for attention deficit hyperactivity disorder and obesity.

(I tried meth for the first time when I was eight. I did it several times as a child. My younger adoptive brother, Ben, has ADHD. When we were kids, he used to hide his pills under his tongue and then spit them out later and give them to me, because I liked them.

I forgot about that until just now, writing this. I've always prided myself on having never touched "white drugs," anything that comes in pill or powdered or liquid form. That's a lie. I just didn't realize it until this moment.)

According to the website of the Garden State Treatment Center, there are seven phases of a meth high cycle:

1. The Rush
2. The High
3. The Binge
4. Tweaking
5. The Crash
6. Meth Hangover
7. Withdrawal

The Rush

When a meth user first injects meth, they feel a "rush" within seconds. During the rush, the heartbeat races and metabolism, blood pressure, and pulse soar. The rush can last about thirty minutes or so.

Methamphetamine is also known as speed, uppers, meth, chalk, ice, glass, Christmas tree, and crank (particularly when injected). It comes in the form of pills, powder, or chunky crystals. Meth makes the user feel euphoric, allowing them to stay up and active for days at a time. It is versatile—it can be swallowed, inhaled, smoked, or injected into a vein. Swallowing or snorting it is called "bumping." Injecting is called a "rush" or a "flash" and creates a shorter, more intense high.

our mother once said she danced for hours in a thunderstorm
barefoot and pregnant, holding petra's hands
she knew it was the only time that we would ever dance,
all three of us.

When I first saw a photo of Petra, I thought she was me. We aren't twins by any means, but we are alike enough to fool each other. Petra doesn't smile as much as me, and when she does, it's a close-lipped, self-conscious smile. Despite the lack of a toothy smile, she laughs more than I do; she is more fun-loving and relaxed than I am.

When I first met Petra, I didn't notice her teeth—or lack thereof. Not when she smiled or laughed. I didn't realize how hard she worked to hide them, the void of them. It wasn't until she asked our mom for a straw for her drink that she explained to me that she can't drink cold drinks without a straw. She has tooth and gum sensitivity, and she was missing half her smile because of what is commonly known as "meth mouth."

According to the American Dental Association:

> "Meth mouth" is characterized by severe tooth decay and gum disease, which often causes teeth to break or fall out. An examination of the mouths of 571 methamphetamine users showed:
>
> - 96% had cavities
> - 58% had untreated tooth decay
> - 31% had six or more missing teeth
>
> The teeth of people addicted to methamphetamines are characterized by being blackened, stained, rotting, crumbling and falling apart. Often, the teeth cannot be salvaged and must be removed. The extensive tooth decay is likely caused by a combination of drug-induced psychological and physiological changes resulting in dry mouth and long periods of poor oral hygiene. Methamphetamine itself is also acidic.

I've never actually seen the inside of Petra's mouth, but she said most of her teeth were gone when we met. I was twenty-one. She was twenty-three. At one point, I think she got false teeth. I write "I think" because I still haven't actually seen them. She pulls her lips over her teeth so you cannot see them, even when she laughs.

In my wedding photos, Petra wears a gigantic turquoise ballgown, competing with the bulk of my wedding dress. (The rest of my bridesmaids wear light, summer dresses in various shades of blue, the hems hanging between knees and mid-calves, as were the directions.)

In every bridesmaid photo, Petra is frowning. She looks like she is going to punch the photographer.

All I remember of her during my wedding is us dancing. We were both laughing and smiling. One of my best friends, Krissy, pulled me aside to say, "If you ever want to know what you look like when you're dancing, just look at your sister."

Petra always says, "Isn't my sister beautiful? I know I'm pretty, then, too, because I just look at her and think, 'That's what I look like.'"

Once, Petra posted a photo of herself on Facebook, and when I scrolled down my feed and saw it, I thought, *Wait, when did I take that photo?* And then I lost my breath. I've never fully understood the term "it took my breath away" until that moment. I thought she was me.

The High

After the rush, the user feels a "high," during which they feel invincible. The user experiences increased confidence and can experience mood swings—mainly aggression. The high can last four to sixteen hours.

Most commonly, methamphetamine is used recreationally due to its ability to instill a feeling of intense euphoria in the user. It is also used as an aphrodisiac, due to its effect in suppression of ejaculation. There is an entire subculture of meth users who subscribe to what is described as "party and play." Party and play participants are mostly made up of men who meet up via the internet for drugs and sex. Meth makes it possible for users to stay awake and sexually active for days at a time before the user must slow down and sleep during the come down. When a meth user experiences a come down, they sleep for days.

petra is named after the damp earth.
Our mother named me after the rain before she gave me up
and let me fade from their memories.

One of the first things that Petra told me the day I met her, the same day I woke up to Lana's infectious giggles, was that the word "*Avalon*" was what the Romans named their gods. When Petra had Lana, she didn't know how to spell it, so Lana's name is Avolan. I like the way she spelled it because I don't like the shortened *Val*. She's always been Lana to me, from the first day I met her to the present day. I love the name Lana because it sounds like her laugh.

The Binge

Binging occurs when the user tries to continue the high by repeatedly injecting methamphetamine. Binges usually last three to fifteen days. During a binge, the addict becomes hyperactive mentally and physically. The user will inevitably experience less and less potent highs until the rush and high completely wear off.

While meth makes users feel invincible, the drug has an extremely damaging effect on the body. Side effects include rapid breathing, an irregular heart rate, increased blood pressure, sweating, headaches, blurred vision, dry mouth, hot flashes, and dizziness. Because the drug often decreases or even eliminates appetite, it has been used as a dangerous dieting strategy for people trying to lose weight quickly. Long-term use can bring on brain damage that causes problems with memory and body movements, mood swings, and violent behavior. When used in larger doses, meth can cause dangerously high body temperature, confusion, convulsions (uncontrollable jerking body movements), and even death.

petra and I have black widow tattoos we got before we knew each other
or maybe, before we remembered.
we are still obsessed with fairies and happily ever after
magic that can change a frog into a prince
and put broken families back together again.

Tweaking

Once the user is no longer able to experience the rush and high of binging, delusions can set in, and the addict becomes more and more dangerous to themselves and others. They may experience an inability to sleep for days and may engage in self-harm.

My sister is absent. She is a dark hole that meth made her. Sometimes I try to reach into that emptiness, searching, grasping for her, wet and raw like a drowned cat. Sometimes I see a glimpse of her in me, like a mirror, or even in my daughters. She has the most beautiful laugh, and kind eyes. Sometimes I see her eyes, before she blinks and fades away. Sometimes she texts me or messages me on Facebook, always from different numbers or accounts. Her children call me, crying for her. Petra and I don't talk anymore, because all I do is remind her of what she tries to forget by doing meth. Last time we talked, I begged her to get her tubes tied. It's so unfair that I cannot have children anymore, while she pops them out (Celeste, Lana, Elias, and Jordan), and then abandons them, like cats do.

Babies who are born to meth-addicted mothers do not show any symptoms of exposure to methamphetamines. In fact, they seem like the best babies ever because they sleep so much. Without overt symptoms, babies exposed to the drug fly under the radar, and it isn't until they approach school age that issues become noticeable, by which time, years of treatment opportunities have been missed, as reported by the Australian Broadcasting Corporation. Methamphetamine is more dangerous to the health and well-being of babies and children than opioids, particularly causing negative behavioral issues in the child around age four or five.

"Petra, Jordan is such a good baby!" I exclaim, on a road trip to bury our birthfather during the COVID-19 pandemic. Jordan is laying on the hotel bed, where I laid him after we brought him and our bags up from the car. Petra stuck a bottle in his mouth, and he was asleep within minutes, even with all the noise and commotion of us talking and putting our things away, getting dressed, and taking showers. Jordan had also slept the entire five hours from Cheyenne to Rapid City.

I am jealous. She is so lucky to get such a good, sleepy baby.

The Crash

The user will eventually crash from the strain placed on their bodies due to the drugs. This is when the addict will sleep for long periods of time. A crash usually lasts for one to three days.

When I first met Petra, she slept all day. She hibernated on June's couch for weeks while June and I took care of Lana. When she was awake, we took Lana on walks and watched movies. I remember June saying that Petra slept a lot. I had no idea why.

I remember watching *Foxfire* starring Angelina Jolie, one of my favorite movies as a teenager. Petra said it was one of her favorite movies, too. That movie will always be special to me; when you don't have many positive memories with someone you long for, you latch on to the smallest details.

A Jolie obsession wasn't our only commonality. While Petra and I didn't know we each had a sister growing up, we both got black widow tattoos, both missing the red ink characteristic of the spider, intending to fill it in later. We've promised not to fill it in until we can do it together. On a whim once in Boulder, we got matching black feathers on our hips.

We both went by the street name Pixie during our rebellious teen years, when we slept on the streets and joined street gangs. At heart, we were still children; we had both been obsessed with fairies since we were very young. I was stripped of my name and changed it to Echo when another street kid pointed out that there was already a Pixie—maybe he knew my sister.

We both ran away to California—Petra made it with Sid, I made it to Oregon City and then turned around because the only bus available that late at night was going back to Portland. I didn't have a Sid . . . I only had myself.

I remember earning the Girl Scout badge for fire making. I made little tin can fires in the front yard and sat for hours, trying to communicate with what I imagined was my long-lost older brother, who was—in my mind—searching for me. When I met Levi, I thought maybe it was him I was missing. In retrospect, maybe it was my sister.

We share the same dreams.
She is a persian queen, bands of gold around her wrists and toes.

Meth Hangover

After the crash, an addict will experience emotional and physical deterioration, feeling hungry, dehydrated, and extremely exhausted. This is where addiction develops, as the user feels that the solution is to get high again to stop feeling so poorly. This period can last from two to fourteen days.

Avolan doesn't laugh much anymore. She's a sweet fifteen-year-old girl—sweet, but troubled. She rebels against her adoptive mother, Alison. Alison is a very uptight, detail-oriented, protective mama bear. I like her. She always seems ready and wound up for a fight. It could be that it's what she's come to expect of my sister, so she expects the same from me.

Lana is beautiful, darker now than when she was small. I've met her once in person since that time when she was signed away. Her hair was a bright, fiery red, almost a highlighter red color. Fire hydrant red. She wore wannabe punk rock gear: too polished to be truly punk, too young to have that real worn-down, don't-give-a-fuck punk rock attitude to really pull off the look. I love her. She's exactly me at fifteen. She has no idea how beautiful and naturally graceful she is. She should be a ballet dancer.

I made her some purple and gold earrings. She wore them the day we met. She barely spoke. We met in a park with my birth mom, Petra, Petra's baby Jordan, Alison, and my husband. It was a COVID summer, and Alison wanted to make sure we wore masks and kept plenty of distance. We only got to visit for an hour before we had to make the long trek home to the Pacific Northwest from Colorado.

During that time at the park, I kept flashing back to the last time I saw Lana as a toddler. I was visiting my birth family and wanted to see Petra and Lana. Petra wasn't coming to June's to see me, so I took it upon myself to venture out on the bus to stay at her apartment one night.

When I got there, it was clear this wasn't the best part of town. There were sketchy guys, half-dressed, covered in dirt, and working on a car outside of Petra's apartment. They checked me out thirstily as I walked by. Petra's door was wide open.

When I walked through the door, I was hit with the stench of old diapers and rotten food. Lana greeted me in only a diaper, crawling around on the grease-covered floor. There was something old and moldy in a pizza box next to her. Dirt and grime and garbage covered every surface. There was no one else in the front room with Lana except the flies. I searched the apartment for Petra and found her asleep with the door closed in the back room.

I stayed the night with Petra, helping her clean and trying to have a heart-to-heart with her. She swore she wasn't using again.

It came out a few days later that she was. It was clear she wasn't able to take care of Lana. Lana wasn't safe. My birth family and I coordinated an intervention and convinced Petra that she needed to let Lana go back to her foster parents so Petra could get some help. Petra cried and pleaded with us to stop, to stay in denial. She knew if she couldn't keep Lana this time, she would lose her forever.

The day that I went with Petra to sign the papers to turn Lana over to her foster parents' custody was the most heartbreaking day of my life. That little baby knew exactly what was happening. She was happy and smiling until the papers came out, and then she started screaming "NO!" and tore the papers out of Petra's hands, demanding to be held, refusing to let go. She knew it would be the last time she would see her momma for a long time.

I remember Petra just let Lana throw the papers. She let Lana throw the papers while she cried, and then she gathered Lana in her arms and held her, their tears combining into little rivers down their cheeks. Petra's long, thick hair fell across their faces like a curtain.

I still see that little girl in Lana. She fights her adoptive mom, resists Alison's efforts to protect her, to bond with her, to keep her safe. She runs away to Petra, time and again, even when Petra disappoints her, over and over. She's a momma's girl, through and through. She never lets go.

Withdrawal

Withdrawal really peaks thirty to ninety days after the last drug use, when the addict has the most tendency to become depressed and experience the lack of energy and ability to experience pleasure. Many users become suicidal at this point. Despite efforts to change, most (93%) addicts end up going back to meth.

According to the National Survey on Drug Use and Health, meth is used by more than 20 million people worldwide. An estimated 1.6 million adults report having used meth during one year in the United States. Over 14 million people in the United States report having ever used meth. Almost twice as many men use meth, compared to women. The vast majority of users are white, and the age demographic with the highest use is 35–49. Most users have a high school degree, but having a college degree makes a person considerably less likely to use meth. The poorer you are, the more likely you are to use meth. Meth use is higher in cities, and using marijuana increases the likelihood a person will use meth.

I know what it's like to hold out hope that Petra will be different one day.

Once, one of those times when she was in prison, she made me a card with a fairy on the front. Inside, she apologized for not being there for me like a sister should, especially an older sister. By that point, I knew better than to expect anything would change, so I kept it for a week or so and then tore it to pieces. I didn't want to hold out hope again just to have it crushed in her palm.

Sometimes, Lana messages me. She doesn't say much. She doesn't open herself up. She just says hello or asks me for money. But I know what she's saying. She's saying she misses her mom, and I'm the next best thing, and I am probably one of the only people who also misses her mom, almost as much as she does. I miss my birth mom, too.

There is something about abandoned babies that keeps us unrooted always, even if we have an amazing new family. Something in us always longs and searches for our cekpa. Something will always be missing.

I hope by the time you read this, things will be different for Petra and Lana. I hope you will grow up to know your auntie in a different way. Petra can be so loving and kind and gentle, and she is hilarious and will always have your back—when she is sober. When she is high, she is simply absent to her family. She never intends to hurt anyone.

If nothing else, I can promise to do everything I can to protect your relationship as sisters, so you will grow up to know each other the way I wish Petra and I knew each other. And I hope you will share some of that sisterly type of love with your cousin.

I am kimimila, a butterfly—she reaches out to touch my jeweled wings
before i disappear again
disintegration.

My Father's Voice

He lived in a tiny house in the middle of nowhere, in "the sticks" of North Carolina, in what was probably once a quaint little home. The once-white, now dusty, yellowish and faded-pink paint was peeling and chipped off, the yard overgrown and wilted in the heat, and the smell from inside permeated the premises as if it had seeped into the very wood of the place. It reeked of stale garbage and deterred dreams.

When he picked me up at the airport, he brought with him his wife, his stepson, and a rusted, broken-down, non-descript junker straight from the rez. He hugged me, and he felt like sinew. I didn't recognize his face; it was his voice, like rolling prairie and sweetgrass and the million bear hugs I missed my whole life.

He called me "baby girl." His skin was like soft, crinkly antique paper when we touched. Like when you are a kid, and you try to make new paper look like an old treasure map by getting it wet and crinkling it and drying it up again. His skin felt like it had been dampened and then re-dried over and over.

He looked like ashes, frail and ghostly in the sunlight. He said it was his liver. He said maybe we could go camping while I was there.

His wife, Luz, was twice his size in both girth and stature, which isn't to say she was a big woman . . . just that he was very small in comparison. She preached the Bible, love, and peace, while her son's eyes bored into my chest, my hair, my lips, my legs, my ass. He made me feel dirty with the way he was staring like he was a starving, wild dog. My dad—I called him by his first name, Eddie—told me Luz's son was dumb now because he got savagely beat in the head with a baseball bat after he raped a girl at a party about a year prior.

I wish he hadn't told me that. I slept in a room with a lock on the door and no windows that night. But even with the lock in place, I still only managed to half-sleep, one eye constantly opening to make sure the door was still closed.

One night, I swear I woke to the sound of the lock turning. I waited, breathless in the dark, watching. I had a very small pocketknife, one of my prized possessions. It was inlaid with Mother-of-pearl and fit into my shoe. I opened it in the dark.

After several moments, when I was sure he wasn't coming in, I reached out and touched the knob. (That's how small the room was, more like a closet. The skinny cot I slept on was on one side of the room, and I could still reach the door on the other side from my bed.) It was unlocked. I turned it back and slept with the pocketknife under my pillow.

I told Eddie the next day. He told the stepson, "If you so much as touch that fucking door, I will fucking kill you. You stay the fuck away from my daughter, and don't you even so much as look at her or I will kill you." That was the one and only time I heard my birth father swear, or yell.

The stepson was in some ways the least of my worries—the house was teeming with cockroaches. They crawled all over me, night and day. They covered the shower, the toilet, the beds, the refrigerator, cupboards. In and out of our juice. I tried not to drink or eat anything. They crawled in my hair and all over my face while I slept. I spent most of my time in North Carolina outside.

We went to Asheville, the nearest town, and walked the hilly streets with the artsy stores and the beautiful colors everywhere. An artist's canvas, wild like a Pollock, the streets were covered in rainbows and grit. I could hear the hill music and taste the Mountain Dew the babies drank deep in the dark woods while secrets went on around them unnoticed. Asheville helped me escape my birth father's house; I was afraid of the crazy men across the street in their wife beaters, sitting on the porch with their shotguns as we drove out onto the street.

My father knew all the street people at the square, mostly men with pot bellies and skinny legs, all smiles and hellos through the haze of their noontime buzzes. Eddie used to be one of them. He used to be all of them. He claimed that Luz saved him.

The night before I left, we went for a walk, a little "father-daughter time." Eddie magically pulled a forty out of his jacket pocket. I had wondered why he would wear a jacket in that heat, even a light one. As the sun pulled itself down from the sky, we shared the cool beer and caught up on the twenty-one years of my life he had missed. He told me his version of his breakup with our birth mom. He claimed my grandfather tried to buy him off. His eyes lit up when he drank; little me's reflected in his pupils against the sunset.

"He told me if I left your mom, he'd give me the truck and a couple grand. Said she was no good, I was no good for her, either." Eddie had affected a North Carolina accent in the twenty years he'd lived there. I told him he sounded like the hillbillies, but inside, I loved it. His voice was so gentle, which is why I couldn't believe what he said next with that handsome accent.

"And Levi isn't my son. Your mom was seeing this guy, this wasichun man. Real tall, good looking. That was between you and our divorce. She was seeing him, and then she stopped seeing him, and we started back up together again. And then she comes and tells me she's pregnant. Levi doesn't look like the rest of you. He's real light-skinned." This much is true. But so is the fact that Levi looks more like Eddie than the rest of us—gray, skinny, medium height, same almond-shaped chocolate eyes. "I guess there's a chance he could still be my son, but I really don't think so."

I took a big gulp of beer and sighed.

"You know I can't tell him that, dad. I'm gonna leave that up to you, if you want to tell him," I said.

It felt like a rite of passage, drinking a beer with my birth dad, him telling me secrets. That was the last time I was alone with him.

The next day, they all drove me to the airport. Luz hugged me for a long time, calling me "sweetie" and telling me how important it was to my father that I had come. Eddie didn't cry. He hugged me briefly and said, "Goodbye, Babygirl. I love you," in that rolling accent of his, and jumped back into the rez car he came from.

While waiting for my flight, I saw a movement out of the corner of my eye and looked. There it was—a cockroach, scrambling out of my bag onto the floor. I almost puked, I almost cried, I almost laughed. Instead, I held it all up inside me and breathed until the moment passed. It felt like a knife, but not sharp, more like a dull pain of anger, and fear, and betrayal, and love, and loneliness, and yearning, all breaking me open and raw, soft and vulnerable. I breathed again and again and again so I wouldn't break completely apart.

I looked around in fear to see if anyone noticed the war going on right in front of their eyes, triggered by the unwanted appearance of that damn roach. No one had.

I got up and walked to another seat, far away.

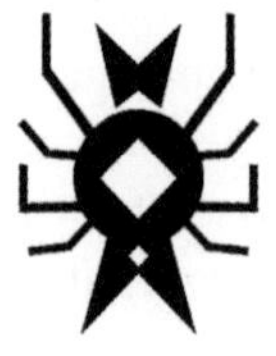

Warm

He sat across from me, your Uncle Sid, hair overgrown and disheveled, with a pane of doubled-up plexiglass in between us, the black plastic phone wedged between his ear and shoulder.

A minute ago, my brother hadn't recognized me with my highlighted hair and dark tan. He had paced the cubicles along the glass, looking everywhere but right at me, until I waved my hand and his eyes lit up slightly before darkening again. He had glanced among the faces on the other side of the glass several times before straightening his orange jump suit and sitting down to pick up the other phone that connected the two of us.

He ran his pale fingers through his shaggy, dark hair. At first, he spoke calmly and clearly—almost too calmly for the Sid that I knew—but his nervous twitching betrayed him.

"Welcome, guys," he said, barely even looking at me while his eyes scanned my side of the room. "I hope you are having a good trip and enjoying yourselves." My fiancée, Logan, held my right hand and waved hello with his free one. I passed the phone to him for introductions. Logan had never met Sid before. I watched their faces; they both seemed calm and friendly. That was a good sign.

When Logan handed the phone back to me, I asked Sid how he was doing and stood up to show him the tattoo that I had gotten with our sister, Petra, two days before. We each got matching black feathers on our hips. Sid and Petra's last name is Blackfeather, as was mine at birth, before I was adopted. At the time of this telling, I was twenty-five.

"That was stupid," he said, aloof. It was originally he and I who had planned to get matching tattoos.

I told him, "No, *you're* stupid," and motioned around me. The emotionless plane of Sid's face cracked for the first time as he laughed in agreement.

"So whose car was it?" I asked. He immediately frowned again and looked away.

"I don't want to talk about that here." He scratched his ear and glanced over at the guard, who was standing to our left near the door back into the inner prison halls.

"What defense are you planning?"

"Well, they are going to claim insanity or something."

"So are you going to the mental hospital?"

"No, I am going to sue them. They have me on a cot in the middle of the floor, in the middle of all the cells, so they can keep an eye on me."

"Really? Why?"

"I don't know. Stuff I said when I first came in. You probably wouldn't believe me . . ."

He was right. I didn't.

It all started months ago, from what I can remember. Maybe even way before that. I remember him mentioning gold even as far back as the very first night that we spoke, the night we first found out about each other and talked until six in the morning. He told me in a whisper about these rocks that turned into gold when you mixed them with some chemicals. Maybe it had started with that.

Then I remember him talking every once in a while about wanting to pan for gold. He said that, when I came to visit them—my birth family on my mom's side—in Denver, we could go to some streams in the mountains. I lived in the Black Hills in South Dakota then, so he asked me questions about Black Hills gold. He said that once, when they were young, he and Petra ran away to California and planned to live on the beach and find gold on the shores to make money to live on. When he was having trouble in college, he called me and tried to convince me to move to Mexico with him so that we could find this special kind of gold in the rocks there.

He tried to turn meth rocks into gold, too, but always got caught before he made any money.

I didn't put it together until he called me one night, months ago, talking about some rocks that he had found while hiking one day. He said they were black and had a silvery sheen to them, and that with pressure and intense heat they would turn to gold. It was days later that I found out he had bought a blowtorch and several gas cans and spent almost every waking hour obsessed with his rocks. June, my birth mother, told me that he lined them up in a row on her front porch and torched them all day long—that he was freaking the neighbors out.

At first, I thought he was high. I was mostly upset at Sid—the worry didn't set in until later on when he didn't seem to be coming down.

When I tracked my birth father down and met him in North Carolina, I gave Sid his phone number and told him that our dad wanted to meet him too, someday. He tore it up and told me he never wanted to speak to our dad again. Eddie had abandoned Sid and Petra when they were little (this is June's version of what happened, the version Sid and Petra were raised with). I thought maybe reconnecting with Eddie would help heal Sid's spirit. I thought maybe it would help him get off meth to know that he was loved still by a father that just didn't know how to be one.

June has severe schizophrenia. You wouldn't know it, though, from the outside. When she's on her meds, she talks and acts like any "normal" person—until you get her behind closed doors and start asking questions. If she read this, June would ask me, "What *is* normal, anyways, Leah?" and stare at me until I look away, uncomfortable and ashamed.

When June starts "thinking wrong," she gets really quiet. That's the first sign, but you wouldn't notice it unless you know her well, since she is normally a quiet person. But then she starts making strange observations: "Did you see that car? Was it the same one that just went down the street a minute ago? Did it look like an unmarked police car?" Then, the inevitable explanation: "There are people still after me, you know." After which, she is unable to communicate effectively, has a panic attack, and must lie in bed for the rest of the morning/afternoon/evening. She can never explain clearly who "they" are, but always seems convinced that "they" are tapping her phone when we talk and can monitor her through the TV. She refuses to touch anything electronic and doesn't own a cell phone or computer. She regards them as if they are covered in a contagious disease that she might catch, a disease that somehow allows the government to monitor your every move.

One time, I asked her, "Would it really matter if they knew your every move? You don't do anything the government would have an issue with, so why do you care so much?"

"That's not the point, Leah," she said, as if I just didn't get it. I didn't, I suppose, and I still don't.

I used to get really frustrated with her bouts of anxiety. It seemed that it always happened inconveniently, like when I needed a ride to or from the Denver airport or when we were all dressed up and ready to go for dinner. Since June doesn't trust anyone using her car besides her, and both Sid and Petra had their licenses revoked years ago, we were always completely dependent upon her to get anywhere on time, unless we planned far enough ahead to take public transportation. Once, I almost missed my flight to get back to Portland, where I was spending Thanksgiving with my adopted family.

Now, I always have an alternate plan. I've learned my lesson enough times, and I don't trust her to come through. Most of the time, she does, but it's that one time that I really need her that she still somehow comes up short. It's become a bone of contention between us, and I have stopped explaining my feelings to her because she can't handle knowing that I don't trust her—even though I think she does anyways. Now I know why Sid and Petra never trust me, or anyone else, for that matter. They have this strong bond between them. They only trust each other.

"Petra said she knew something was wrong," says June after I am back in Portland from visiting them. We are both silent, the old house phone on her end crackling in the distance between us. "She said she's known for months now that he isn't right."

I wonder if maybe the drugs have something to do with it still, as if it would be any better to know that my brother is high on meth all the time instead of losing his mind.

"When are they letting him out?" I ask, playing with the edges of the blanket across my legs as I think. The week before, when I visited him in prison in Fort Collins, he had been there for over a week already. He should have come down by then, if it was meth that had temporarily made my brother insane. Even after I flew to Colorado to see him for myself, I felt even more confused about what he was in for, why he had stolen a car, and what had made him press on the gas instead of the brakes when a cop attempted to pull him over.

"I don't know," June's voice is husky and filled with emotion. I could see her in my mind, graying mid-length hair framing a reddish-brown face, small dark brown eyes like mine, thin lips, and high Persian cheekbones. When we left, she was so depressed about Sid that she couldn't even eat dinner at the same table as us and cried nonstop. "His court date is tomorrow. I guess we'll know then. I wish I didn't have to do this."

"I wish you didn't have to, either."

A week later, Sid was sitting across from me at a Mexican restaurant in northeast Portland. He told June that his probation officer gave him a release to leave the state and come to Portland to try to get into the university where I was going to school. She believed him. I didn't.

"Bullshit," I stated over the Latin beats and rowdy bar, while we hashed out his story over tacos and strawberry margaritas, all on my dime. "You're a convicted felon. And that was *before* you stole the car!"

When he called me an hour earlier from downtown Portland, asking me to pick him up from the Greyhound depot and help him find somewhere to stay, I tried to keep the panic out of my voice.

After hanging up, I thought to myself, *food first*, and left work a little early to get him. *The least I can do is feed him before I convince him to go to the loony bin.*

My objective was clear—get Sid some help. I called June on the way downtown. She said that she was sorry; she had tried to talk him into going to counseling right when he got out of prison while waiting for his court date, but he would have none of it. She gave him the money to come see me as a last-ditch effort. She couldn't handle him or his rocks anymore and hoped that I could talk some sense into him. First, I had to get him to trust me.

So I listened. I sipped my drink, then another, and another as he talked.

"Do you really want to hear this?" he asked before beginning. "You won't believe me," he said again.

It went something like this:

He stole the car because he was running from the KKK, who had infiltrated Longmont—where he lived with June—and had a mission to kill all the male descendants of Crazy Horse.

Why not the females? I asked.

"Why would I know, Leah? Are you sure you really want to hear this?"

I nodded, although I wasn't.

Well, so . . . Sid stole the car because he saw a guy who he thought might be a part of the KKK group that was hunting him. He thought this guy was going to kill him because the guy "wasn't acting right." The guy kept looking at him like he was watching him and then was talking on his cell phone, probably to keep the other KKK members informed of Sid's whereabouts. So Sid made a move towards the guy as if he had a gun and was going to shoot, and the guy seemed scared at first but then just kept walking like nothing was going on when he realized that Sid didn't have a gun. Weird, huh? That's what Sid thought. So he went to the store to get a drink, and thought it was weird that these other people at the car wash across the street were watching him, too, as he went into the store. Sid started to get creeped out, because it didn't seem like anything was real anymore. So he said a prayer: *God, if this is real, and I am really alive right now and not dreaming or in an alternate reality or something, please show me a sign.* To further test this unreality, Sid took a soda out of the cooler in the store—it was a Pepsi . . . no, a Mountain Dew—and then just walked out. He just walked out. He didn't pay; he just left. And no one stopped him. Weird, right?

So because these dudes were watching him and then he had this feeling of unreality and he prayed to God and stole the Mountain Dew—no, Pepsi—from the store and nobody stopped him, Sid determined that this reality may not actually be real. Then, the strangest part occurred. As he was walking out of the store, Sid noticed a truck that had its keys inside. Sid thought, *Now, why would there be such a nice truck with the keys inside, just ready for someone to steal?* He walked on thinking that things were getting weirder and weirder. *Then* he passed another car—it was black, and shiny, he can't remember what it was, though . . . probably a Camry—that had its keys inside, as well! Now *that* wasn't a coincidence! But he kept on walking across the street. He sat on the curb and waited for five minutes while he drank his Pepsi, praying to God, *God, if you want me to take that car, then when I go back in five minutes, let the keys still be in the ignition.* And they were.

Sid was caught three days later, speeding down the highway, just returning from the reservation in Pine Ridge after looking for any men in our family who were also descendants of Crazy Horse to warn them about the KKK group that was trying to murder them all. After several other cop cars got called in on the high-speed chase, they finally resorted to laying down the strips on the highway that have spikes on them to pop the tires on the stolen car.

"It was great, Leah," he told me. "I picked up these two hitchhikers before I got caught, and they were egging me on the whole time. They kept saying, 'Go, go, go!'"

I paused, then laughed, deciding to play along as if everything he had just said was completely normal. As he talked, I felt my brother slipping away from me like coarse, glittering sand, cutting through my fingers as he blew away from me forever.

After dinner, I drove him to Providence hospital and refused to leave until he had checked himself in.

Five days later, I received a phone call at work.

"I want my stuff back."

"Sid?" I asked, confused. "What are you talking about?"

"My stuff. I came with a garbage bag of clothes and a pillow, and I left it in your trunk last week. I need it back. I'm leaving."

"What? Why?" My heart dropped. Despite the sinking feeling of the past few days that he was one step out the door already, I had prayed and hoped that he would stay and work with the counselors. I had been visiting him almost every day, bringing him brand-new clothes, books, fresh underwear, and even a radio. I made sure June and Petra called to check on him. I argued with his counselors and doctors after Sid stopped cooperating, trying my damnedest to convince them—and him—that he knew he needed help and was willing to do the work.

"I'm not crazy."

After arguing with him, I finally conceded to come outside during my lunch break so that I could give him his supposed bag.

"Sid," I told him over the phone, "if you do this, if you leave the hospital, I want you to know that I am not going to support you doing anything other than getting help. You are sick, and you need to be in some kind of treatment."

He came at lunch, as promised. I was in a meeting. When I met him at the front office, the look on the receptionist's face said it all. *Get this crazy person away from me!* I led him outside to the parking lot.

Sure enough, in my trunk was a white plastic garbage bag that smelled like dirt and mold, and something sour that I couldn't quite place—something between urine and puke. I lifted the bag between my forefinger and thumb and scrunched my nose.

"Here you go."

Sid took the bag as I slammed the trunk shut. We stood there awkwardly for a moment.

"So . . ." I folded my arms. "What are you going to do now?" I had already told him that he couldn't stay with me. I really believed he needed to be in serious, full-time treatment and therapy.

"I don't know." His brows furrowed as he looked down, not meeting my eyes. "I guess I'll just go sleep at some homeless shelters or something, if I can get in." I didn't respond.

"Well, would you give me at least a blanket or something if I have to sleep on the streets?" he asked. "You could at least do that for me."

"Sid." It was a statement. "You had a bed, free meals, and the help that you need. And you left." I felt like there was a heavy weight on my chest.

It was one of the hardest things I've had to do. I said, "Yes, of course I would give you a blanket . . . but beyond that, I can't help you, Sid. Not until you are willing to help yourself."

He shifted from foot to foot and then coughed in the ensuing silence. He lifted his bag over his shoulder and started to walk away.

"Well, then, Leah." His voice got hard. "Have a nice life."

"You, too, Sid."

As I walked the other way, back to my work, he said, "Thanks for everything."

The sarcasm cut neatly through me, a knife in my chest.

I paused, looking back to watch him leave. He was wearing the thick green sweats and hoodie that I bought him earlier that week, a long-sleeved white thermal shirt I had also bought him, and the dirty old shoes he was wearing when I made him check into the hospital, minus the shoelaces. When he checked in, they'd asked him to take off his shoes so that they could remove the laces. His black socks had holes in them and smelled like he had worn them all week. He had been so embarrassed that he threw his socks in the garbage and tried to wash his feet in the sink to get rid of the smell.

As he walked away from me now, he hitched up his sweats, and I saw the heavy-duty gray socks I had brought him to replace the ones he threw away.

He didn't look back, not once. My proud, strong, crazy brother walked away from me, alone.

Resilience

I remember the group therapist's name—Rudy. I will never forget his name. There was very little we'd actually spoken to each other that was not directed to the entire group, but out of the handfuls of therapists I've seen in my life, he made the biggest impression. And I can't decide how I feel about him—if he was an absolutely brilliant therapist, or a terrible one.

Rudy was tall, thin, and very light-skinned, with medium-brown, chin-length hair. I remember him wearing a lot of brown. His entire aesthetic was just brown—bland, like his personality. But I guess his job wasn't to have a personality. It was to study us, to find out what made us tick, where our points of pressure were, and then experiment to see if he could make us explode just so that he could show us how to put ourselves back together again. He was, ultimately, a scientist, and we were his specimens.

I approached group therapy sessions like I had approached my master's degree program. Other than the two years of high school that I blew away drinking and using, I've always been an overachiever, a straight-A student. I'm a visual learner and an avid reader, so I remember just about everything I read (but don't talk at me, it goes into one ear and out the other). I read ahead and do all the extra credit. I almost always know the answer when questions are posed to a group, so I can fly under the radar with just about everything else. Instructors know that I am on top of my coursework, so they don't worry about me during class.

The rest of the group were in different places in their lives. Most of them were younger than me, and they came to the program from court orders or straight out of inpatient treatment centers, detention centers, or mental health facilities. One girl spent her entire first group session scratching deep trails into her forearm with her nails, which made me itch. I used to lick the blood after I cut; watching her, I could taste the metallic sweet liquid.

When we came back from break, she was gone.

"She isn't ready for group," said Rudy. No shit. It had been almost a decade for me, but that girl made those scratches look delicious.

I didn't like Rudy. He was very cold and clinical. He rarely cracked a joke and didn't care for conversation. He wasn't the least bit impressed by my charm or my ability to stay ahead of the rest of the class; however, he paid little attention to me because I was a model student. I spent most of the time looking at my phone under the table, texting my husband and friends, researching wedding décor, and arranging a viewing for my wedding dress. Rudy didn't seem to mind as long as I paid enough attention to answer questions and participate in group discussions.

Rudy also had what I considered a bullying streak. If one of the group participants seemed "off"—angry or anxious or bored or antsy or stressed—Rudy would single that person out, find their weak point, and press on it until they broke. One person broke down crying in class; another had an outburst, threw a chair, and had to be removed. Rudy seemed almost giddy when he got a reaction, almost the only time he really seemed to be enjoying himself, with his mean little smirk. Afterwards, he talked to the group about what happened, assessing better ways to handle the situation by employing Dialectical Behavioral Therapy (DBT) skills.

I mostly stayed under his radar, but I knew my luck had to run out eventually. One day, it would be my turn.

After Sid's appearance in Portland during his psychotic break, I worried that something like that could happen to me. I was in my mid-twenties, and in researching my brother's condition, I discovered that psychotic breaks leading to schizophrenia most commonly happen during a person's late twenties or early thirties.

Other factors leading to a psychotic break include substance abuse and extreme stress.

I had just graduated with my first master's degree, and I didn't have any downtime. I was planning a wedding, working as a full-time grant writer in a nonprofit organization, and I had taken on a lot of student loan debt. Saying that I was stressed out was an understatement. Sid's appearance threatened to push me over the edge. I decided it was a good time to do some preventative treatment.

When I was a teenager and experiencing episodes of depression, my parents put me in an outpatient treatment program called the Portland Dialectical Behavioral Therapy Institute. DBT is a specific type of cognitive-behavioral therapy that teaches a variety of skills to help people cope with stress, regulate emotions, and improve their relationships. While DBT was originally intended to treat borderline personality disorder (now not even considered a real diagnosis by many mental health professionals), DBT has been adapted to treat other mental health conditions, such as eating disorders, substance abuse disorders, and post-traumatic stress disorder. Techniques include group therapy, individual therapy, and over-the-phone coaching.

I attended the Portland Dialectical Behavioral Therapy Institute (PDBTI) the first time when I was fifteen, during a time when I was experiencing intense anxiety and depression that caused me to go from being a straight-A student to completely failing and not even attending classes. I started drinking regularly and using recreational drugs to cope with the stress and anxiety. I got kicked out of school and my soccer team, and I was a treated like a pariah by the majority of the kids at my high school freshmen year. Part of the problem was that I had never been in a large public school before. I had always been homeschooled or in very small private, religious schools. I was ahead academically, so I was in classes with kids that were older than me and more socially adept. I had terrible, extreme social anxiety, and I didn't know how to interact with the kids at my school.

Instead, I developed relationships with kids on the outskirts of the social circles, kids who were struggling socially, like me. We skipped school together, preferring to drink and use and make out with each other in the park or at someone's home while their parents were at work. I ran away from home with these kids, multiple times, crashing on couches or staying out all night partying. We were the misfits, and we pushed each other to see who was weirder, wilder, crazier. I won on those fronts multiple times.

After an inpatient stint in a psych ward and an outpatient rehab facility at age fifteen, I was referred to PDBTI for intensive outpatient services. The focus of PDBTI is on the development of "core mindfulness" skills, which are based on techniques used in meditation that help a person focus on the present, or "live in the moment." Core mindfulness draws a person's attention away from negative thoughts, feelings, sensations, and impulses, using the five senses to tune into what's happening around them in nonjudgmental ways. The result is the development of healthy coping skills which can help a person stop engaging in automatic negative thought patterns and impulsive behavior in the midst of emotional pain. Other skills addressed include distress tolerance, interpersonal effectiveness, and emotional regulation.

The first time I went through PDBTI's substance abuse program, I was a teenager. I showed up to each and every one of my one-on-one therapy sessions and refused to talk to my therapist, Brody. If I did, I did so in one-word answers. We sat there, for an hour, in silence. I studied his fancy shoes, his khaki pants, and his plaid shirt. Although his wardrobe was that of a middle-aged man, his face betrayed his age; he looked only ten to fifteen years older than me. I felt he was trying too hard. He was actually kind of cute, with his light-skinned baby face and fresh, short haircut. He seemed clean and safe—but so different from me. How could he ever understand any thoughts going on in my brain?

After the first session, Brody started talking to me. He told me things about himself. He asked me questions, gave me prompts. The third session, he eventually told me to leave if I wasn't going to use the hour. The fourth session, he asked me if I wanted to go get ice cream.

I nodded yes.

While we were waiting for ice cream at the Dairy Queen down the street, he asked me questions about myself that had nothing to do with my feelings or substance abuse or why I was in therapy. I began answering his questions as I licked my cone while we sat on a bench in the sunshine. I had always loved the butterscotch dipped cones from DQ; my adoptive father always got those for me growing up, particularly on trips to the beach.

Talking was easier after that.

One time, he asked me about the cuts on my arms. I usually wore long sleeves to cover them, but it was hot that day, so I just tried to keep the inside of my lower arms facing towards myself. I remember the air conditioning in his office was so cold, I held my arms against myself for most of the session. Yet, somehow, he saw them.

My response was, "Animals engage in self-harm by rubbing their bodies against trees or other items in nature until they bleed. They do it when another animal they care about dies or when they are hurting."

What I meant was, *It's natural. It may not be "normal," but I'm not crazy. I'm just hurting.*

Normally, people lectured me about cutting because they were afraid of it. They thought it meant I was suicidal. I've had a couple of suicide attempts, but when I cut, I wasn't suicidal. It made me feel better. If I wasn't drinking or using drugs to cope, cutting helped. I knew it was because it released adrenaline and dopamine and serotonin, just like drugs. I was addicted to it. I felt so much better after one or two cuts. What made it even sweeter was knowing it was "subversive," something seemingly scary that people misunderstood—exactly the way I thought people felt about me. (And I was okay with that.)

Brody's response had nothing to do with judging me or telling me that what I was doing was wrong.

He said, "You know, you can get the same exact effect if you hold an ice cube in your hand as long as you possibly can. And you won't scar up your arms. Wanna try it?" I did. And it felt just as good. I can't remember cutting after that. I held ice cubes, instead.

But that was not the last time I drank.

I got clean and sober the first time when I was sixteen. It took a few times, and then eventually I found a great circle of friends in their teens and twenties who supported each other's sobriety through AA; we met primarily at a late-night AA group and then spent all night out at 24-hour cafes, playing chess and talking about our sobriety and spiritual practices.

My longest period of sobriety was four years, from ages seventeen to twenty-one. I was in AA, did all the steps—twice—and got deeply involved in Lakota ceremonies. I called myself "straight edge." I still got piercings, tattoos, stayed out all night, and slept with whomever I felt like sleeping with, but instead of alcohol, I drank coffee. I didn't miss weed or pills much. I honestly didn't miss drinking at all. But when I went away to college, I didn't want to miss out on the parties and the fun I heard about.

From twenty-one to twenty-six—all through college and then my master's program—I partied hard and made up for all those years of not drinking. Honestly, I had a blast. I loved my life. But instead of cutting, I started depending on alcohol to get me through the hard times, as well as make the fun times more fun. I was never fully dependent on alcohol, or what you would consider a true alcoholic. In fact, I went without alcohol for several weeks or months at times, when I thought I was overdoing it or when I was trying a new diet or lifestyle. But I always went back; it was a cycle.

Enter Sid. Seeing my brother go through a legitimate psychotic episode, like our mom, scared me shitless. I never wanted to lose myself like that. I knew that substance abuse and stress were major factors in their psychotic breaks, and I knew I needed help figuring out better coping methods.

So in my mid-twenties, I remembered PDBTI and Brody. I realized that I hadn't absorbed everything there was to that program when I was fifteen and thought, *maybe there is something more in it for me.* I looked up the program online and asked for more information.

I wasn't expecting the waitlist to be so long—six to nine months! I was lucky to get fast-tracked and ended up only waiting for three. I went through the intake process and realized right away that the PDBTI therapists were used to dealing with people more in crisis than me. Cliché questions like "do you hear voices?" made me cringe. The intake process made me feel more sane than anything, but I was committed to going through the entire outpatient treatment program if it meant that I would be less likely to end up schizophrenic or with other major mental health issues.

My new therapist—we will call him Jeff—was very sweet, very kind and patient, much like Brody. He dressed like Brody, too, and was about the same age—a younger white guy with nice hair and teeth, the epitome of clean-cut.

After the intake, Jeff said, "You obviously have PTSD, and that's what we are going to focus on during our one-on-ones, but that group is full, and I think you would benefit from our Substance Abuse Group Therapy sessions." He went on to explain how I was far from an alcoholic, but I did engage in self-medication via alcohol use to cope with stress, anxiety, and emotion regulation.

"Our goal is for you to develop skills other than self-medication to cope with challenges in your life."

I sighed and rolled my eyes. From my years in AA and other treatment programs, I staunchly believed that treating the underlying issue is the key step in treating the addiction. And from my research on adoption and years of therapy, I know that I have childhood PTSD from the adoption process, and that the way that PTSD has affected my brain and my mental health has been something I've struggled with my whole life.

"Fine," I said. "It can't hurt, I guess."

It was close to the end of my time in the program (the second time around)—I think the second-to-last week before I graduated. The entire time I was in the program, I was multitasking, holding my phone just under the lip of the table so that I could text.

Rudy had never mentioned anything about my texting until that second-to-last session. He held that shit close and waited for just the right timing to confront me.

"Leah," he said, tilting his head in that emotionally distant way of his, studying my behavior. "Is there something more interesting going on with your phone than this class?"

I shook my head, turning it off and sticking it in my pocket. "Nope."

He hesitated, then shoved his hands deep into his khaki pockets, pursing his lips and leaning his shoulders slightly away from me.

Uh oh, I remember thinking. His shit-starting pose. I knew it was coming.

"Why don't you share with the rest of the group? What is so important?"

I laughed, uncomfortably.

"I'm good."

His dark brown eyes searched mine, holding the tension.

"Well, since you can't seem to focus on this class, why don't you hand over your phone?"

Like a child. He was treating me like a child. I was a nonprofit development professional. I had a master's degree. I was getting married. And I was only doing this program as a preventative measure. I didn't *really* need to be there.

I wanted to lose my shit. I wanted to, so bad.

I took a deep breath, staring him down. Then I handed over my phone.

"You can have it back at the end of class."

I spent the rest of the class fuming. Rudy called on me for almost every question. He asked for my thoughts and opinions. Every time I spoke up, he challenged me or asked me for an example to share with the class.

The air was potent with the sense that I might lose it at any minute, but I was determined not to break.

At the end of the class, I asked for my phone back. He handed it over without looking at me, as if I were nothing to him.

During a person's last class in the program, the tradition was for all the other participants to go around and say one positive, empowering word that describes that person.

During my last class, I didn't look at my phone. I told myself, *just suck it up and get out of here.* I was actually looking forward to seeing what people thought of me. Rudy always participated, volunteering his word last. I was very curious what he would say about me, given that our interaction the week prior had not been positive.

I don't remember much about what anyone else said about me at the end of the class; most of it was expected, standard, things we all said about each other: kind, smart, funny, friendly. We went around the circle, and then it was Rudy's turn.

I expected him to say something barbed with negative meaning, something to put me down, shame me, in a passive-aggressive way. I steeled myself for that feedback. Like any other negative thing people have said about me, I readied myself for the punch, prepared to receive it with stoicism and ennui.

He held the silence for a long moment, his head in his hand, elbow on the table, thinking.

He looked right at me, but like I was an intriguing anomaly, not really a person.

"Resilient."

Years later—after the wedding, after I completed my master's degree program—I ran right into Rudy in an upscale natural grocery store. I was with a friend from work, and she and I were filling up on snacks during our lunch break, chatting animatedly and laughing.

As we turned the corner, his lanky frame came right at me. We both stopped suddenly, and then I looked up. Our eyes caught, briefly, recognition hitting us both at the same time. He looked exactly the same—same haircut, same brown plaid button-down and light-brown khakis.

I hesitated, my breath catching. I opened my mouth to speak. He barely shook his head; it was imperceptible to anyone but me. And then he walked around me, as if we were strangers. I continued around the corner, with my friend, giggling at her story.

I didn't much like Rudy. But he changed me. He gave me a gift. He helped me to see that I am stronger than I realize.

I've thought about this for many years. In the years after my recovery period in AA, my years of involvement in spiritual ceremonies, getting my high school degree and then my associate's through the

Gateway to College program, and finding my birth family, I've been asked to speak to groups of teachers, parents, and students about my experiences. The one resounding question I get is some form of "what makes you different? What is it about you that made you succeed when others fail?"

I spent many years as a grant writer for nonprofit organizations that focus on families and youth. I've done a lot of research on a children's resilience. The negative things that happen in a child's life are called risk factors; the more risk factors a child has—homelessness, an adult with addictions, divorced parents, poverty, a marginalized race—the higher chance they will experience challenges to their long-term success. However, protective factors—such as a positive role model or homework support through an after-school program—can mitigate those risk factors and increase the likelihood of a child overcoming the challenges they face in life.

One of the greatest protective factors for a child is a sustained, long-term connection with a caring adult. While I have been through adoption—which research has shown to affect a baby's brain in very negative ways—and while my upbringing wasn't perfect, I did have many strong relationships with members of my adoptive family. Together, they helped raise me in a loving, caring environment, an environment in which I thrived.

I was lucky. I won the jackpot in my adoptive family. Not every family is like that. Not every adopted child experiences a safe childhood filled with love. I know that.

Research shows that even if a child does not have a safe, loving family, they can still thrive with caring, healthy relationships outside of their home. That's why it's so important for adopted children, children in foster care, and children experiencing challenges at home spend time with loving family members outside the home, or other caring adult mentors. These people are so instrumental in building protective factors for a child, so that when they get to young adulthood and adulthood, they have more of a shot at success.

Regardless of how loving and wonderful our family is, we are not perfect. Your father and I are far from perfect, as I'm sure you will know well by the time you read this. The rest of our family isn't, either. But as much as we struggle, I do know without a doubt that you are surrounded by love.

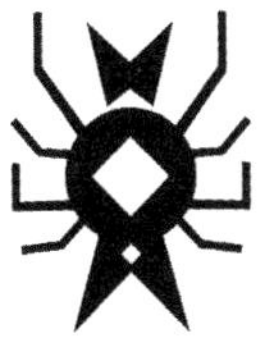

Two Ones Coming Together

When I was fourteen, I liked cruising by a toy store in the mall called All Wound Up—the one with the cute older teenage boys standing at their post right outside the store, walking the dog with their yo-yos. One day, my cousin and I chatted up one of the boys at the front, who turned out to be the manager. I was too young to work retail in Oregon, but I wanted to make my own money so I could actually afford to buy the lipsticks and earrings and candy my cousins and I stole.

We liked the nice mall in the suburbs the best, the one with the upper-middle-class girls with their North Face hoodies and Coach purses. My cousin and I dressed like chola girls with the big hair and heavy makeup, old plaid shirts of our dads' tied around our torn-up jeans. Crystal taught me how to draw on liquid eyeliner real thick so I looked *at least* sixteen.

Danny wasn't that cute, actually, and he was at least nineteen, much too old for me. But he was an older boy, and he had a job—a manager job, no less—and he was the ticket to getting a real paycheck. So I flirted. He showed off, spinning the yo-yo around his head (Around the World), and zipping it towards my stomach, pulling back at the last second before it hit me. I asked if he had a job opening, and he took me to the back room to fill out the paperwork while Crystal browsed the shelves of toys.

He asked a lot of questions, wanting to know where I went to school and what I liked to do for fun. He was very chatty, standing too close and taking his time with the paperwork. Finally, he handed me an application, offering his desk so I could fill it out, leaning over me while I bent my head. His cologne smelled musky and dangerous. I felt the adrenaline in my toes.

"You're sixteen, right?" he asked when I hesitated in filling out my birthday.

I looked up at him, batting my thickly lined eyes and flipping him a saccharine smile, "Of course I am, silly." I added two years in my head and wrote the date—1983. Now I was a liar and a thief.

A few weeks later, I confided in one of the older girls that I was actually fourteen. She had suspected and cornered me one day, treating me like an older sister would, acting concerned about me. One of the new boys had taken me out in his Camaro the week before after our shift—top down, loud bass and rap reverberating my ass in the passenger seat, like an elicit massage. We got dinner at the Applebee's next to the mall, and he kissed me before dropping me off at the bus stop. He was eighteen. I didn't know if he actually believed I was sixteen, or just wanted to.

He was angry when she told him. He reported me to Danny. Danny called me into the back room the day after my coworker spilled my secret.

"Okay, so we are in a pickle," he said, shoving his hands deep into his pockets. "I should have checked your ID. I didn't, because I believed you. That's my bad." He looked down. "But why would you lie to me?"

I felt terrible, but he was also at fault. He didn't check my ID because of his crush.

"The easiest thing would be if you just quit. I can have your paycheck ready for you to pick up tomorrow." It was only my second or third check.

I agreed. When I came to pick up the check, the boy with the Camaro refused to speak to or even look at me. The girl who had squealed glared me down from her corner of the store. Danny handed my check over quickly, eager to get me out of there for good—disaster averted.

A few months later, I passed by the space in the mall where All Wound Up had existed for less than a year. It was vacant. Christmas had passed, and the store struggled until finally giving up. I wondered what happened to Danny and the boy with the Camaro. I've had a penchant for sports cars and loud rap music ever since.

My husband is a walking contradiction. One of the things I love the most about him is that he surprises me.

I swear I've always known we were supposed to be together. I just didn't realize it was Logan in my dreams until almost a decade after we met.

When I was probably about eight or nine, I saw my future. I knew, deep in my bones, that my person would be tall, dark, and handsome, with dark hair and medium-brown skin. I was obsessed with boys who had L names. I used to repeat them in my head . . . Logan, Luke, Landon, Liam, Lance, Lyle, Lennox. When I was a teenager, if I ever met a guy that matched that profile, I would do everything I could to catch his attention.

Your dad was different.

Logan seemed more like an older brother at first. He was lanky and tall, with glasses and wild, curly hair. His wide grin was in a perpetual smirk, and there was always something always up his sleeve, some terrible dad joke on the tip of his tongue. He teased me relentlessly; it annoyed me and drove me crazy.

My first day at Oaks Amusement Park (my first legal job), he taught me how to flip burgers, clean the grill, and cook fries in the huge vat of hot oil. I burned my hand severely, and he held it under cold water while I screamed. Our boss moved me to the cotton candy stand.

I chopped off my hair one weekend before work and dyed it pink. I had bleached and dyed it so many times, it was like straw and broke off when I so much as ran a brush through it. Cutting my waist-length hair down to two inches was the only option, and I felt free. People came up to buy cotton candy from me more than anyone else because they wanted to buy it from the "girl with the cotton candy hair." My fingers tasted like spun sugar every day when I got off work. Sometimes I didn't notice it was all over my hair, like spiderwebs, because it was the same color. I felt like a sugar plum fairy in my pixie cut and small frame, glitter all over my cheeks and eyelids.

Logan got promoted to skate guard in the skating rink, and our boss moved me to the rink when the summer season ended. I was lucky to be one of the kids she kept in the off season.

When the concession stand was dead, I'd watch Logan skate, complicated dance steps I couldn't even attempt to emulate. He was a pro at "rexing"—his skates wove back and forth, crossing each other, first the right foot in front, and then the left, while he sped around the rink. He'd negotiate with me to put on the chipmunk mascot suit for kids' birthday parties; in exchange, he cleaned the grill and took out the garbage. I always acted like I hated the Chipper suit, but the truth was, I hated taking out the garbage more than any other task at Oaks Park—the full garbage bags were almost as big as me and leaked.

A group of our coworkers—Lyle, Dylan, Emma, Corine, Logan, and I—went through Oaks Park's haunted house after work one night and then drove together to a party at Logan's parents' house. All the older carnies were there, drinking and smoking late into the night. I remember learning to play poker at their kitchen table.

That's also when I learned that Logan drove a Camaro—dark shimmery teal. Logan and Lyle and I rode to the party in the Camaro with the top down. He had a police scanner and raced through the suburb streets, blaring Eminem, keeping one ear out for the scanner.

Up until that point, I thought he was such a square. That night, I saw a flash of a different side of him.

Unfortunately, we didn't get to know each other much better than that, because I got myself fired. I was getting in trouble at school, drinking and smoking and skipping classes, and they told me not to come back. I was sent to an alternative school in North Portland, on the other side of town from Oaks Park, and had to catch three buses to get there and home every day. I didn't have time to get to work all the way across town before my shift began. I didn't see Logan again for seven years.

After school in South Dakota and my internship in DC, after traveling across the country and back to find my birth family and immersing myself in their lives and perspectives, I craved the comfort of home. Not just my family and the home I grew up in—I also missed the cold rain and the way the rich earth of the Pacific

Northwest smells against the backdrop of leaves and air, so clean you can taste the minerals in it. I missed the beach and feeling slightly damp all the way down to my bones, in a way that makes a hot bath on a rainy day or curling up under a thick blanket with a book the most delicious feeling. I needed to look out my window and see trees. I needed *home*.

I registered at Portland State University and got a small on-campus studio apartment. All of the apartments on the PSU campus were located in buildings made in the '20s and '30s, tiny rooms with dainty kitchens in separate areas, with space for a tiny bistro table, all the wood original and painted white, naturally distressed throughout the years of college renters. There was a little coat closet off the main area and a cute little bathroom with one-inch porcelain black-and-white tiles and a cramped little tub with a shower attachment. It was perfect.

I decorated with dried flowers and little trinkets from home, a little wood-and-glass table and old loveseat from Goodwill near the front door, a small two-person kitchen table in the five-foot dining space. I cooked all of my meals on the stove and didn't own a microwave or a TV. My bed was a single futon that lifted up into couch.

It was the first time I lived alone my entire life, and I loved it. I relished the hours spent alone in the quiet, reading or doing homework. If I wanted to watch a movie, I'd rent a DVD and stick it in my laptop. If I wanted to socialize, I walked across the street to the closest on-campus bar, where I'd inevitably run into someone from a class or student government or the gym. I kept myself busy working for the school paper and student government, participating in clubs, working out, and playing adult rec soccer. On weekends, I'd take the MAX to the eastside, across the river to Parkrose, where I would visit my family. Having my parents, brother, grandparents, aunts, uncles, and cousins all living on one street made visiting everyone convenient.

Right away, I reconnected with my family and my old high school friends. They all had so many questions about my birth family and my experiences. I spent many evenings having dinner with my family and then hanging out with high school friends later on at night.

I came home to find my car no longer in its space in our driveway. When I was in South Dakota, my brother Ben had killed my car—something about grinding the gears too much. My best friend,

Audrey, from student government at Portland Community College, had her own apartment in Parkrose and her own car, so she'd come pick me up from my mom's to hang out. We would drive around town, going to bars to play pool, or we'd meet up with the guys we knew from our community college days.

Audrey had a thing for one of my best guy friends from high school—David. Anywhere David was, she wanted to be. She'd drag me to meet him and a group of guys at Tik Tok Around the Clock on 82nd and Powell in the middle of the night, or to go listen to him and his friend Mike sing bad karaoke downtown. I knew since high school that David had a crush on me, but we had never dated. He was like a brother to me; I had friend-zoned him long ago.

One night, Audrey called me drunk, crying, saying that she had thrown herself at David, and all he could do was talk about me. She made me promise I would never date him.

Eventually, she stopped chasing David and fell in love with a sweet boy named Ronnie who adored her.

I was dating a boy named Juan who lied to me all the time, but whose mother and sister loved me. They paid my way to visit their family with them in Guatemala, and Juan's sister gave me a very expensive purse and satchel set for my birthday, for the trip. I was never in love with him, and I knew it was long past time for both of us to move on, but I loved his family too much to let go. I swore to myself I'd break up with him first thing after the trip. I tried to leave him in Guatemala, in the middle of downtown Guatemala City, and then quickly realized that I was not safe without his presence in that country. When we got home, I took all of his things out of my apartment, lugged them down the four flights of my building, and left them in the lobby for him to pick up.

A few nights later, I was lonely and sad, and David asked if I wanted to play some pool at my favorite pool hall. He must have sensed I was vulnerable, because he did all the right things—he let me win a few games (he was a better player than me for many years), he bought my drinks, he complimented my outfit and hair without making it awkward, and when I was sufficiently tipsy and happy, he put my favorite song on the jukebox and spun me around, literally sweeping me off my feet. I remember looking at him in a different way, thinking, *when did you grow up?*

When he dropped me off at my apartment later that night, he asked to come up and use my bathroom, and then he stayed. He was exactly what I needed right then: someone familiar and comforting, someone I knew loved me.

The next day, he asked me to come to his house with him, offering to make me food. We drove back out to the Parkrose area, and before we got out of the car, he said he had something to ask me.

He stuttered at first, his hands shaking.

"I- I- I was just wondering . . . if like, maybe what we did last night . . . You know, maybe we could do it again?"

I thought it was about the sweetest way I'd ever been asked to be someone's friends-with-benefits.

"Oh, yeah . . . of course!" I said, wanting to get the awkwardness out of the way. "Yeah, of course we can keep doing this. This is probably exactly what I need."

Then he asked me to stay the night with him at his place. And then the next night.

He lived with two of his brothers, and he introduced me as his girlfriend.

Wait, I thought. *That's not what we talked about.* But in a way, I was flattered. He was one of my closest guy friends, and I knew he loved me, had loved me forever. Maybe it was okay to let him be my boyfriend. I mean, how many movies are there about best friends who become lovers?

He asked me what my favorite flowers were—stargazer lilies—and he bought them for me every week, when the last bouquet had wilted. He drove me everywhere, telling me I didn't need a car, because I had him. He worked a night shift delivering papers all over the Portland metro area and Vancouver, but he was always available when I needed a ride. If I didn't text or call him right after his shift, he would call me. If we weren't talking on the phone, he wanted to be with me all the time.

At first, his attention was flattering and addicting. I never had someone want to be with me so much, someone who seemed to want to inhale me whole. He seemed to crave my touch, and he complimented me constantly. He wanted to feed me, to buy me things, to give me gifts. He introduced me to female friends of his and then stared at me while we talked, flaunting his adoration in front of them. There was nothing I could possibly do to upset him.

He was an amateur photographer and loved taking photos of me. We'd go to the beach or hiking in the forest, and he'd take photos of me in front of sunsets or splashing in the waves or in front of giant trees. Sometimes he would pose me, like a doll—like his puppet.

At that point, I was accustomed to being alone. I started to miss coming home to an empty apartment—and staying there. Alone. Of reading alone in the quiet while sipping tea and listening to the rain fall. He never left me alone long enough to think.

A few months in, I started pulling away, insisting on time to myself. He'd react terribly, as if I were rejecting him because I wanted to be home with my cat some nights. He started taking his friend Sarah with him as a companion on night shifts, making sure I knew she was with him. He'd cancel plans with me to hang out with another female friend of his, or he'd make sure I knew he returned a gift he was going to give me. We'd fight horribly, and then inevitably make up and be together again 24/7 for days, until the cycle started again.

He insisted on setting up a bank account for me under his name, which he deposited money in from each of his paychecks. I told him not to do it, and I never touched that fund or asked him for money, but he told me every time he put money in or took money out for gifts he bought me or trips he paid for. He gave me an ATM card, "just in case," and then when we fought, he texted me to tell me that he withdrew all the funds.

It wasn't long before he started lashing out physically. He never punched or slapped me, but he pushed me, picked me up high into the air and slammed me into a couch so that the wind knocked out of me, and held me under the water once in a swimming pool for so long I started breathing water. I started seeing a counselor, and when I brought him with me once, she said that his issues were too deep for her to treat and referred him to someone else. He never went. I started going to a domestic violence support group.

Our relationship didn't last long—a total of maybe eight or nine months. But it scarred me. Finding my birth family, while a positive thing ultimately, was traumatic, and it had left me raw. My relationship with David took me over the edge.

Looking back, I am surprised at myself. I've always thought of myself as empowered, as a feminist, as a tough girl. If it had been anyone else, I do not think I would have let it get that far. During that time, I kept coming back to the fact that David was my friend. I'd known him since we were kids. We went to freshman year of high school together and kept in touch through my years at college. I was his friend when his mother shot his stepfather and went to prison. I knew his mom before that; he knew mine. We ran away from home together. I knew about the abuse he and his siblings suffered at home. I knew how he threw himself in front of his sister when his dad went after her. We took care of each other.

I knew his demons, and for some reason, I thought I had to be the one to cure him. Like, maybe if I loved him enough, it would make up for all the things that had happened to him before me.

It all ended one night when he stalked me home from a dance club. I went with some friends from school, including some guys he knew, so he knew where I was and what I was doing. He came running at me from behind when I opened my apartment door and shoved me across the room. He proceeded to grab the Christmas gifts we bought our families together that I was storing, slamming me against walls and doors and the coffee table when I tried to stop him.

I tried to call the police, but he grabbed the phone out of my hand and took the SIM card out, shoving me to the ground to keep me from reaching my phone. Something switched in me when he did that. When he ran out the door, I got up and ran after him. He was at the stairs when I caught up with him. I pushed him as hard as I could.

Luckily, he caught himself by grabbing the banister as he fell down the stairs. He turned and looked up at me. The strangest thing—he looked like *I* had betrayed *him*. I felt victorious—I was finally fighting back. It was like a lightbulb in me came back on, and I remembered who I was . . . the tough girl who I held back for the duration of our relationship. She came out swinging.

He came back a little later "to return the SIM card" he had stolen out of my phone. I was sobbing, looking for my cat who had fled the scene, when he knocked. When I heard his voice, a deep, dark rage burned up my belly and exploded out of my mouth. Screaming, I grabbed the closest item to me on the floor—my keys—put each key in between my knuckles, opened the door, grabbed my SIM card out of his outstretched palm with my free hand, and flung my fist at him with everything I had. He pulled back just in time for the keys to barely graze his cheek. I slammed the door and locked the bolt.

The next time I saw him, it was in court. I had appeared in front of a grand jury, and they charged David with assault. His lawyer pled it down to a misdemeanor. Because he threw me through the threshold of the apartment door before he entered the apartment, they had to drop the felony. The law isn't always fair, but I won, and he wasn't allowed within 500 yards of me, my home, my workplace, or my school.

My cat hid in the closet for days while I moved to a new apartment. When I finally found her, a few days later, she was starving and scared, afraid of me, even. I promised her, and myself, that we would never be in that position again.

That night, the campus police came to document the scene. While no one came out to help me, plenty of neighbors heard me screaming and called it in.

They decided to remove me from the apartment for the night while they found me a new on-campus apartment in a different building. I could move in the next day.

I remember that a snowstorm was brewing, the wind whipping the trees around all evening. It was so cold, and I worried about my cat. I didn't know where she went, but the officers hurried me along. I packed a bag of essentials and took one more look around before I left.

An officer drove me to the nearby University Place Hotel. I remember walking in the door with my oversized gold Baby Phat bag from Juan's sister, dried tears staining the makeup on my face, looking up into the eyes of a cute boy at the front desk. He wore a uniform like the officer standing by my side, different from the other hotel front desk worker. He was obviously a security guard, but when he saw my police escort, he stood up quickly and asked how he could help.

His eyes were gentle and completely focused on me. He had a smirky grin that looked more kind than cruel, and he had broad shoulders. He stared at me as the officer gave a quick overview of the situation and checked me in.

His laser attention made me uncomfortable, so I looked anywhere else. My first reaction was attraction, but after what I'd just been through, I shied away from him. *Oh, no, buddy*, I thought, *Not so fast. Not tonight. I've had enough of your kind.*

The officer got another call and headed out while the security guy finished checking me in. When the cop left, he spoke in a low voice that only I could hear.

"Hey," he said, as he ducked his head a little to catch my eye. "You don't remember me, do you?"

I looked up, surprised, searching his face for something familiar. I shook my head.

"Logan. From Oaks Park."

I gasped, covering my mouth.

"Logan! Oh my . . . You look so different!" He wasn't the teenage boy I knew from before. He was still thin and tall, but he had filled out, bulked up in the arms and shoulders. His face was longer, with deeper angles, a more defined cleft chin and cheekbones. He was very handsome.

Again, I felt that pull, a gentle tug that threatened to draw me to him as we talked, catching up on the years since the last time we saw each other, when I came to pick up my final check at the skating rink and told him goodbye through the window at the front door.

He walked me to my hotel room and told me to let him know if I needed anything. He said that he'd be watching the front all night and doing rounds to check the hotel grounds, so I would be safe. It was so comforting to see a familiar face and know he would be there all night so I could sleep without worry.

The room was frigid, with huge floor-to-ceiling windows at the back of the room. I lifted the cover on the ancient heater and turned the knob. Nothing happened.

All I had was thin pajamas and an outfit for the next day. There was no way I would be warm enough to sleep through the night.

I called the front desk. The other hotel worker answered, "This is Levi." I asked if someone could come turn on the heat.

A few minutes later, a knock on the door. It was Logan. He had that smirk again. My heart flip-flopped. I brushed it aside. *No*, I told myself firmly. *The last thing I need is another guy mucking up my mind again so quickly.*

"I'm sorry," I blushed. "I just can't figure out this old heater, and it's freezing in here." I clasped my hands in front of the jacket I was still wearing to emphasize the temperature of the room.

He went to the heater, flipped a couple of switches, and turned the knob down a little bit. He turned around as he stood back up and grinned, crossing his arms across his chest and squaring his feet and shoulders, like a cop. He seemed to be poking fun at me—still that teasing older boy underneath the years and uniform.

We chatted for a bit, and then I told him I needed to get some rest. Having a guy in my room the same night my ex had thrown me around my apartment was making me nervous. He said goodnight and told me to let him know if I needed anything else from him, in that same mischievous tone like some subtext I didn't understand.

When I woke up the next morning, late, there was a note slipped underneath my door.

> *Hey, Leah,*
>
> *It was good to catch up with you last night. It's been a long time!*
>
> *It sounds like you've been through a lot. If you ever need someone to talk to, feel free to email me at...*
>
> *Sincerely,*
> *Logan*

I giggled to myself. I never had a guy give me his email address, but not his phone number. It seemed almost antiquated, like asking someone to write you letters.

In retrospect, if he had given me his phone number, I never would have called. I might have texted, but it was unlikely. Given what I had been through, email seemed less threatening. So I did email him that night.

We exchanged long emails for weeks before going out to lunch in person when I found out he was on-again in his on-again, off-again four-month relationship. A couple weeks later, we planned a double date. I was hanging out with another ex-boyfriend at the time, and Logan was still seeing his girlfriend, though the threads of that relationship were quickly unraveling. We went to a comedy show and then played pool after, but Logan and I were the only ones who knew how, so we ended up playing a few games while our dates pouted at the table together. When we left, Logan's date grabbed my date's arm and asked him to walk her to the car, since Logan seemed more interested in me than her.

A couple of weeks later, he texted me, telling me that their relationship was on the rocks again.

Well, then break up with her and start dating me, I texted back.

That night, he took all of her things back to her that were at his apartment and asked me out to dinner and a movie.

Battle Buddies

The paintbrush swirled orange and red and yellow and white—fire colors—around my friend Abby's eye, curling around the arch of her brow and curving down her cheekbone. I dipped the tip in a palette of glitter and traced the outline of the butterfly wing with it.

Right before I did it, I was suddenly hit with a jolt of unexpected nerves. As I laid out the paint and supplies, I realized I didn't actually know how to paint faces. I'd never done it before. However, we had it planned for months now, so there was no going back. It was an hour before the wedding, so this was go time.

When our best friend, Samantha, announced her wedding theme was "Surrealism" six months earlier, we had to Google it. Odd, artsy, strange, eccentric, weird, strangely beautiful . . . We decided to attend the event dressed as butterfly ladies in long black dresses, glittery face paint, and butterfly hair adornments.

Finishing up my face paint, a butterfly in blue and purple covering the half of my face opposite Abby's, I admired my work. I had taken a CBD gummy about an hour earlier, and it was just starting to hit. I know those things aren't supposed to make you high, but I'd be damned if that glitter didn't seem to dance right off my face.

We topped off our look with the hair butterflies, grabbed our purses, and walked out of the hotel room we were sharing in the little bed and breakfast inn Samantha rented out for the event. She and her new husband, Doug, had already held the wedding ceremony the day prior, long before any of the guests arrived. They opted for a tiny ceremony and a weekend-long beach party, instead.

After a short after-wedding ceremony in the courtyard, where I inappropriately burst out in a weird laugh/cry (further proof CBD does get you high, after all), we were ushered in with the larger group of family and close friends to the most awe-inspiring dinner I've ever attended.

Acrobats twirled and flipped in the air above our heads, where we dined on a fancy catered surf-and-turf dinner, with the finest wine in crystal goblets. The small, intimate dining area was dark and mysterious, all heavy drapery and red and gold tones. A strange magician with fake eyeballs hanging from his hat made his way around the table to the chairs where Abby and I sat.

"Butterfly lady," he said to me as he approached. "Pick a card, any card." I drew the three of diamonds. "Now just stick it in this stack, anywhere you want, facing down." I did so. "Now take the stack." I did. "Shuffle it." I shuffled it. "Now hand it back." I handed the stack back to him. "Okay. Is this your card?" He tapped on the top of the stack, lifting the first card. Three of diamonds.

Seemed legit enough. Pretty cool trick. But what he did next was amazing.

He drew on Abby's hand, an eyeball, with a black Sharpie. Then he had her close her hand and slammed it against his own closed hand. He opened his hand, and there was an eyeball, drawn in Sharpie. He had her open her hand. The eyeball was gone.

I started to feel all fluttery. The magic and acrobats distracted me, but this whole night was leading to an apex, a moment I had been waiting for . . . actually, for years.

The toast.

As our meal came to a close and the desserts were handed out, the acrobats finished their final acts, and the magician sat down at the table next to us to eat, removing his eyeball hat so it won't hit anyone in the face, somebody started a chain of dinging glass against metal. *Ding ding ding!*

My stomach hit the floor. My hands were wet. I took a sip of water and breathed deeply.

Someone had appointed himself emcee of the evening and asked me to speak. I stood up.

"The first time I met Samantha, I was the executive assistant at the Native American Youth & Family Center. My office was next to the front office, and I remember walking inside, and this strange hipster chick was sitting there. She said something like, "Hi! My name is Samantha!" Really perky and happy, which is not how we Indians usually run things. We are stoic. I thought, "Ugh, stay away from her."

"But as I got to know Samantha better, I realized that she was very useful. She knew all about implementing processes and procedures, and she was really smart and quick. If I asked her something, she would do everything in her power to find out the answer. She was amazing at graphic design and photography, and she designed *many* flyers during her time at NAYA. But still, she was an outsider, and she wasn't Native, so I wasn't sure about her.

"However, I remember the day I decided she would be my best friend. We were sitting in the front office, and she mentioned she was having a hard time trying to do something with her hands because one of her hands was messed up. When I asked her why, she told me she fought off three men with machetes in Africa because they were trying to take her purse. They had chopped her friend's hand almost completely off, and Samantha fought them off in an alley and also got her hand sliced, so one of her fingers doesn't straighten out.

"When I heard that, I decided then and there that Samantha would be my best friend, because I know that if we are backed into an alley and have to fight someone, she will have my back, no matter what."

Seven years prior to Samantha's wedding, I was having a wedding of my own.

There isn't really a way to have a wedding in my family without having at least 60 family members attend . . . just on my side. Not even counting his family, or our friends. And we couldn't really have a wedding party without *all* of our friends, because if we invited one to be in it, the other would get jealous.

So that's how we ended up with 150 attendees in my grandma's backyard, in the far back of the property, behind the pool, in the gazebo. We were the second-to-last wedding that old gazebo saw, the last being my cousin Derek and his wife Jaime, who married a couple years after us.

The ceremony and the photos, the bouquet toss, and the garter toss . . . it was all a blur. I appreciated the advice of our photographer prior to the festivities. She insisted on doing the wedding party photos long before the ceremony, which was being held in the heat of the day on a Saturday in August. I just wanted to make sure there would be no rain.

"You should eat now before everyone gets here."

Best advice the entire wedding.

There was a lull between the photos and the dinner, and I went to find Samantha to help me use the restroom. I wanted a short dress but got talked into a long, unwieldy princess gown with a train. I needed help.

I walked into the little ADU my parents built in the back of my grandma's house, which served as the wedding party's dressing and hang-out area.

It was quite a sight. Brushes, bags, makeup, hairspray, champagne glasses, were all scattered about. I followed a trail of discarded women's shapewear to the bedroom.

Samantha was sitting on the edge of the bed, downing a glass of champagne, her makeup smudged, tears streaming down her face. A pad of paper was on her knee, and she had a pen in her hand.

"Honey!" I exclaimed. "What's wrong?"

Samantha set down the glass and glanced at me before looking down at her paper.

"Oh. This?" She said, nonchalantly. "I'm trying to write my maid of honor speech."

She looked away from my face, an O of surprise made of my mouth.

"Samantha! You're going on *right now*."

She sighed.

"I know," drawing out the *O*. "I thought I could wing it."

"What are you going to do? I need your help going to the restroom right now, and then we are up."

"Well, I guess I'm going to have to wing it, then. It's okay, I think I know what I'm going to say."

A few minutes later, I ended up cutting her speech short, frantically motioning my flat hand like a knife across my neck. *STOP STOP STOP!*

When Samantha noticed me, her eyes got big with recognition, realizing that, in her well-intentioned, last-minute, alcohol-induced effort, she was about to tell a *very* inappropriate story. She stuttered and sputtered, then vaguely referenced the idea of battle buddies in the military, stating that Logan and I are more than best friends, we are battle buddies.

Here is the story she was going to tell.

Two years earlier, Samantha and I organized a camping trip on the Oregon coast with our boyfriends. We invited a few other friends, but they didn't work out. On a last-minute whim, we invited our younger co-worker, a young woman named Julie, to join us. We knew Julie had a boyfriend named Carlos, but we had never met him.

We got there in the afternoon on a Saturday and got camp set up, ate dinner, and sat enjoying a fire. We had a couple beers, nothing too crazy. Samantha's boyfriend, Loren, brought a guitar and was singing to us at the fire. It was very chill, lazy, satisfying. We had discussed, hours earlier, that Julie must not be coming.

An old Honda bumping gangster rap interrupted our revelry. It pulled up in the spot next to us.

"Is that them?" I asked, rolling to stand from leaning on Logan, who was laying on his side. Logan jumped up and followed me over to the car.

"Hey guys!" announced a jolly voice, as the driver opened his door. Julie peeked her grinning face out the window.

Slowly, a huge, burly Mexican man unfolded himself out of the tiny car. He stood up, swaying, and stretched upwards, a bottle of tequila in his hand.

"I'm Carlos! Pleased to meet you." He set the bottle of tequila on top of the car. We all came up and shook hands.

Carlos then began pulling more bottles of liquor out of the car, setting them next to the tequila. Whiskey, vodka, mixers.

Whoa, this guy knows how to party! We were still in our mid-twenties, so we didn't think anything could go wrong. Of course.

"Let's go to the beach!" he yelled, grabbing the bottles. They hadn't even set up their tent yet.

Samantha and Loren, a bit older than us, peeled off from the group not long after we got down to the water. They could see trouble coming from the way Carlos was drinking.

Logan and I, always a little more reckless, a little less self-protective, and younger, stayed to take shots with Julie and Carlos. We sat and talked for a while, watching the waves under the moon. It was bright, even at night after dark on the beach.

Soon, I had to pee, so Julie and I decided to head over to a few straggly trees for cover. As we turned to walk away, I heard Carlos say to Logan:

"You better go rape that bitch or I'm going to do it for you."

When we got back, I told Logan I wanted to go back to the campsite. As we walked away, I told him I heard what Carlos said.

"You should have said something, Logan," I insisted. "You should have told him to fuck off."

Logan stopped abruptly in the sand.

"You want me to go tell that 400-pound, six-foot Mexican man to fuck off? Do you know what would happen to me?" He laughed.

Tipsy off the shots, I wouldn't let it go. It was the principle of the matter. Logan should have called Carlos out.

I shoved Logan, and Logan shoved me. I fell in the sand. Carlos and Julie were a bit behind us at that point but were catching up.

"Fine!" he yelled. "You want me to do something, I will."

Turning around, he walked up to Carlos, looking upwards at him. With no hesitation, he raised his voice and said, "You need to tell her you're sorry for what you said."

"What?" Carlos stopped, raising his hands and looking around. "Are you serious? For what?"

"For saying you were going to rape her. You need to apologize to her. And to your girlfriend, too."

Carlos hesitated, processing what this small stranger was telling him to do. Julie crossed her arms, pissed as well. We all stared at him, waiting.

Then he leaned his head back, opened his mouth, and laughed. He laughed a deep, body-shaking laugh.

And then suddenly, he lunged forward and punched Logan in the face. Logan's glasses flew off his face and into the sand.

I knew he couldn't see much but dark shapes without his glasses. Once he righted himself, he crouched, feeling around for them.

That's when Carlos grabbed Logan by the neck and squeezed, one-handed.

The last thing I remember is dropping my beautiful new Coach purse on the ground. I'd never had anything that nice or that expensive before, and I cherished it. I remember looking down at it on the ground and feeling very sorry.

What Logan said he saw was the shape of me launching myself at Carlos, knocking his arm away from Logan's throat, and then climbing up Carlos's shirt, my right fist flying.

When I came to, I was on the ground, and Carlos was standing above me, his hands covering his nose, yelling, "Bitch! You broke my nose." I scrambled off the ground as he came towards me. He grabbed me by my jacket and lifted me into the air.

Logan had found his glasses and came up behind Carlos, pulling him away. Carlos grabbed Logan's neck again.

"That's it, I'm calling the police!" I screamed. "You're going to kill him." I called 911. When Carlos heard me talking to the operator, he let go of Logan and started running, yelling at Julie to follow him. June ran after.

They spent that night in the woods. They didn't come back until around midday. When I woke up, I looked over at Logan next to me in the two sleeping bags we had zipped together in our tiny two-person tent. He had bruises all over his neck.

"Carlos really could have killed you," I said, as Logan opened his eyes. He nodded.

"I'm so sorry," I said, laying my head on his chest, kissing his bruises. "You were right."

He patted my back.

"Samantha taught me that in the military, they get paired up, and the person you are paired with is called your battle buddy. If you are in battle, you protect each other with your lives.

"This is the idea she was trying to convey *at my* wedding when she was my maid of honor. I found her frantically scribbling her speech in the bridal suite, tears streaming down her face, her shapewear discarded on the floor. When I asked her why she was crying, she said she was worried she wouldn't do justice to all the memories we've shared.

"She then proceeded to throw water all over my dress during my first dance, yelling "It's raining. It's a good omen!" And she kicked wine glasses into my grandfather's garden, where they shattered.

"Despite all of that, I knew her intention was to share her love for me. However, that day, I *vowed* to roast her at her own wedding.

"So, I have a story I want to share. For my bachelorette party, our other best friend, Abby, convinced us to go to Vegas. On our very first day there, we rented a party bus that took us to all the best dance clubs. It ended at the most exclusive club in Vegas at the time . . . however, we were told at the beginning of the tour that we needed to be at the last club before 11 p.m. in order to get in. We were late by five minutes, and when they wouldn't let us in, Samantha who is very liberal—started protesting. She shouted at the bouncers about our rights, kicked over a stanchion, and then sat down Indian style in front of the club—in my short leather dress she borrowed—and refused to move. They had to close the doors and lock them because she was making such a scene.

"Our friend Krissy, who is very sensitive, started crying. Abby, who is the mom of our group, started yelling at Samantha to get up. I looked at the scene and simply turned around and walked out the door. Abby came running after me, grabbed my arm, and said, "Leah, you better get back in there and make her get up right now!"

"I sighed, turned around, and went back in the door. I walked over to Samantha, kneeled so we were eye-to-eye, and said, "Samantha, do you trust me?" She looked at me, and her whole body relaxed, and she said, "Yeah, I trust you." She took my hand, got up, and we walked right through the door into a taxi.

"The bachelorette weekend ended with Samantha and I sleeping on the floor of the airport, Krissy engaged to a guy we met in the pool, and Abby yelling at us that she was going to leave us in Vegas and never to speak to any of us ever again.

"The point of this story is that this is my best friend. We trust each other fully, so when one of us is getting off course, we can tell each other to get back in line. We can go for months without speaking, and I know I can still call her anytime, and she will be there for me.

"At my wedding, she intended to share that VERY INAPPROPRIATE story because she wanted to share an aspect of my relationship that she admired. She wanted to tell everyone about how my husband and I are battle buddies. But I think it's a good thing to have more than one person who will have your back, and this girl is my battle buddy, too.

"Even when we drive each other crazy, or make mistakes, or embarrass each other, we are there for each other, and these crazy experiences that seem like a disaster at the time are the ones that we tell again and again. We relive them, and they make us laugh, and cry, and feel. These are the stories that make the greatest memories, and I'm so happy to say that most of my greatest memories involve this girl right here.

"And Doug, I'm so happy to share my battle buddy with you. She will always have your back, and she will help you make the best memories.

"Cheers!"

It is true that Logan and I are battle buddies, but our scars go deeper than a drunken fight with a 400-pound Mexican guy due to a miscommunication.

At the time of this telling, at Samantha's wedding, Logan and I had gone through the deepest, darkest time in our relationship and were just barely coming out the other side. Unfortunately, that timeline coincided with the births of our daughters—particularly, our first. What was supposed to be the happiest time of our lives started as the hardest.

Aurora, none of this was your fault. In fact, you are the reason we survived. You are the reason that we decided to repair the damage we had done to ourselves and each other. You gave us a higher purpose, a reason to keep walking along the path of our marriage to accomplish our dream of having a family together made of both nature and nurture. You and Acacia saved us, for we would have surely died, in one way or another.

I don't know how to write this in a way that is charming or scenic or pretty without dredging up issues from the past that almost destroyed us, or without making either of us look like horrible people. And I refuse to air my husband's dirty laundry in such a public way—his story is his own to tell, or not tell, as he wishes. The best I can do is hold myself accountable for my own actions.

My husband is charming in a cowboy kind of way, a hold-the-door-open-for-old-ladies kind of way. He has a laid-back, easy way about him that attracts men and women alike. He listens (or seemingly listens). Although he is not a pushover, he knows how to appear accommodating, which is disarming, particularly to women who feel unheard or unappreciated. He and I both know how to make people feel good about themselves.

Sometimes, people get the wrong idea. They confuse kindness with attraction. They latch on to the person who makes them feel good about themselves.

Coming out of an emotionally and physically abusive relationship in which my ex used his female friends to hurt and control me, I viewed every female friend of Logan as a potential threat. And while some of them weren't, some of them truly were; I didn't know which was which because everything about them was veiled from me. Neither Logan nor I knew how to have healthy relationships. My reaction was to return an eye for an eye, and up the ante.

People who have been adopted, no matter their age, commonly have attachment issues. They are either very attached in a codependent, unhealthy way, or they tend toward the other extreme. In my case, I swung back and forth, and when confronted with any potential threat, I bailed. I would sever the relationship before the other person could. I would intentionally break it. I could cut off friends, family, significant others, and not look back once. The coldness, the numbness, that followed, scared me. I sometimes felt like I could do anything and not feel anything at all. I felt broken. I could make anyone not matter to me, including myself.

I've broken up with my husband at least twenty-five times since we first started dating. I've broken all of his dishes. I've even broken

DVDs. I've thrown every insult I could at him in an effort to make him leave me. I've made him get on a plane in the middle of the night to fly home from Denver. I've started fistfights with him. I've kicked him out of my car; I've jumped out of his car and ran off in the middle of the night, scaring him.

There was only one time that he gave up on me. That began a three-month separation in our marriage, when we both licked our wounds and dated other people.

Shortly after we officially decided to separate, I found out I was pregnant.

Chasing the Auroras

Logan, I texted. *Did you hear about the auroras?*
Yeah! he responded. *You can see them from the Gorge right now, right?*
It was the night before New Year's Eve.
Let's go find them, I wrote back.
Like right now?
Yes, right now. I can't go in my car, we'd need your truck. And we always said we would chase them if we could. I really want you to see it.
Okay, he replied. *I'm on my way.*

He picked me up in his dark grey Chevy he just purchased the month before, just a month after we separated. We stopped at a gas station on the forty-five-minute drive up I-84 to the lookout above the Gorge, not far from Multnomah Falls. I bought a pair of warm gloves and thick men's hiking socks and those little heat warmers they keep up at the register that you can shake and put in your gloves or pockets or socks to keep your extremities warm.

Logan kept saying he was going to put one of those bars across the bottom of the truck so I could step up more easily into the passenger seat. It was already getting awkward to bend at the waist...he brought a step stool for me, just in case, and hovered in case I fell on the ice. His hand under my elbow was warm and comforting and familiar, and yet . . . the waters we were navigating were unchartered, casting a new and unfamiliar light on every movement, everything we said to one another, like strangers, but we weren't.

We got hot chocolate at the gas station store; I mixed mine with coffee. Logan drove us to the lighthouse, passing cars stuck on the side of the road, sometimes in the middle. He had chains and 4-wheel drive, so we glided past them all to the top.

The air was the kind of cold that made everything look sharper than normal. The sky had an eerie navy blue-and-green glow to it, the edges almost yellow. The stars were so bright, they looked surreal, like an edited *National Geographic* photo. It was so beautiful, I wanted to smoke a cigarette, mar that moment with something bad, to breathe in the sharp chemicals with the sharp air, both freezing my lungs at the same time.

"How have you been?" he asked.

"I'm okay," I responded. "I am hungry all the time, but I feel too sick to eat anything. My back hurts every time I play pool. I don't know how I'm going to keep playing four nights a week."

We laughed. I had been playing on four teams for years at that point, out at bars four nights a week or more. My life was about to change drastically with the baby.

"I don't know how I'm going to do this by myself," I continued.

"You won't be alone," he said.

"I know, but it's not the same. This isn't the way I imagined it."

I told him about the guy I had been seeing. Austin. He had a daughter, Gia, and was separated from her mother, Veronica. Austin and Veronica fought horribly over everything having to do with their daughter, and Gia had witnessed domestic violence from both her parents multiple times at the age of seven. One night, when Veronica saw me at the house, she tried to attack me, running around the house, punching and kicking the doors and windows, screaming. She kicked in the back door, and Austin shoved her out of the house . . . she fell on the steps and called the police, saying that Austin had attacked her. As she swung her car out of the parking lot, she sideswiped my silver Mustang GT, causing me two hundred dollars in damages.

"This happens all the time," sighed Gia, as I tried to distract her with the fancy mini cupcakes I had brought her and her dad. I held the cupcakes so tight I squished them, trying to stop my hands from shaking.

"I don't want that for our child," I told Logan the night he picked me up to take me to see the auroras.

"We won't be like that," he promised me.

We stayed out there until 7 a.m. After a while, we stopped talking and just enjoyed the moment of calm in the eye of our storm. We never saw more than a tiny, bright-green glow above the gorge for just a moment.

I asked him if he wanted to go with me again on New Year's Eve, but he said no. Instead, he went to a party with his friend. I brought a girlfriend with me, instead, and blocked Austin's number when he called me, repeatedly, drunk, apologizing for something he said.

When Logan and I first started dating, I was still reeling from the terrible relationship that came before him. I was also still processing my experience moving across the country to find my birth family. Before our wedding, Logan's father passed away. Then, our baby died. This was our first baby, two years prior to our separation. (Or can you really call it a baby yet, when it was the size of a gummy bear?)

I was only nine and a half weeks along when I went in for my second checkup. I was twenty-eight years old, three years after we got married. Since about the time we got married, I begged Logan to have a baby. He wasn't ready, so we waited. Then, we stopped waiting.

He was with me when the technician conducted the ultrasound. I remember the walls were so white, no windows, sterile. I remember staring up at the ceiling while the technician poked and prodded. Suddenly, she got very still.

"Your doctor will be in shortly," she said, as she calmly set down the imaging wand, stood up, and walked out the door. I stiffened.

When the doctor came in, I took one look at her face and knew. She prescribed pills that would help my body rid itself of the dead fetus. I held it all in until we were waiting in the lobby for the prescription. I burst into tears, and Logan held me against his chest and whispered in my ear, protecting me from the stares of strangers.

That weekend, we were attending a leadership retreat. We went anyway. I woke up in the middle of the night in excruciating pain. At first, it just felt like I had to take a massive shit. But then that feeling increased until it felt like I was going to split into two, ripped right up the spine. I rolled around the bed, crying—no position helped. Logan begged me to take the pain medication they gave me.

Nobody tells you how it feels to have a miscarriage. You hear all the birth stories, but no one tells you how painful it is to lose a baby.

I discovered that walking helped. I paced in our little retreat room, back and forth, for hours. When I felt my body expelling pieces of my baby and placenta, I stopped to use the in-suite bathroom. I couldn't bring myself to look in the toilet bowl. I just took deep breaths and focused on managing the pain and staying grounded.

That morning, I made breakfast for everyone at the retreat and gave a presentation on leadership approaches. I had only two hours of sleep and was still bleeding profusely. I never went to the hospital. I read many online support group posts about miscarriages, and I kept watch for the signs that I needed to go to urgent care or call an ambulance.

Despite the pain and trauma, I felt calm. I trusted my body to know what to do.

Logan didn't tell me until a week later that his mother learned she had stage 4 cancer. He found out while I was miscarrying, and he held it inside until the miscarriage was over.

It was too much. We both fell apart. We both fought and turned away from each other, seeking solace in other people. In a way, it's exactly what we had to do, right or wrong. We had to separate in order to work through our pain and find ourselves again, find each other again.

It was a slow coming together, one that took a lot of time and healing, Logan and I unknotting the tangles of our marriage, laying the threads out straight, braiding and unbraiding and braiding back together again.

We were still healing when he accompanied me to our five-month check in, when we got to find out the sex of the baby. I was so sure it was a boy I didn't even consider another option. I was carrying low, everyone who said they had a "sense" about these things said so, and I had even done all the activities spawned by old wives' tales, like hanging a pendulum over my belly to see if it moved side-to-side or up-and-down. I had already bought boy things—an adorable blue knitted sweater with a tiny hood, little boy moccasins, a gray Navajo rattle.

I remember the look on Logan's face when he found out we were having a girl. His eyes got wide, frightened, like a deer in headlights. Watching his reaction, I burst out laughing. I laughed so hard my eyes watered.

"You *so* deserve this! You want to be surrounded by women all the time . . . there you go."

He was in denial for a week, asking the doctor and all of the midwives at the birthing center what the likelihood was that they were wrong.

I wanted to name her Kimimila—"butterfly," in Lakota.

"She could go by Kim, Kimi, Mimi, or Mila!"

Logan made a sour face, "Nobody will be able to pronounce her name. I won't be able to pronounce her name."

We finally agreed on the name Aurora, because of the night the auroras started to bring us back together. The calm in the eye of the storm for us, the night of possibilities, the night when we put aside our differences to chase a dream.

The day of the baby shower was crisp, bright, and sunny—everything a beautiful spring day in May should be.

Logan and I were sore and tired, but happy. I had helped him install large pieces of exquisite slate in our backyard patio, squatting and lifting and repositioning . . . probably much more hard labor than I should have been doing at seven months. But I felt good, strong. I also planted a garden in a planter box Logan made, and a larger one with a lovely metal frame with a stylized gate and trellis, picturesque vines already spiraling in between the metal bars.

We set up a BBQ in the new patio so that people could just go around the house without having to go through it, dragging in dirt and the pine needles prevalent in our area of Portland, where several pines grew in our front yard. I spent every single day sweeping and vacuuming that house, all 2,175 feet of it, to no avail. By bedtime, there were needles all over the floor by the door, again.

"Welcome, welcome!" we exclaimed as more and more people showed up. I had followed the event rules I was taught in student government—always invite triple the amount you expect to actually show up. Most of my friends were party friends, pool friends, friends who didn't have kids . . . I never thought they would all show up for a Sunday baby shower. And yet, they did.

The sky darkened as the backyard filled. The mood was still jovial, but it quickly turned when the rain came suddenly pouring down. Then, the thunder, rolling; you could feel it coming up from the ground. We rarely have such storms in mild-weathered Portland, but that day was an exception. Lightning filled the blackened sky as Logan started BBQing the meat, hoping we could appease our growing crowd with beer and burgers. The newly dug patio began to fill with water, soaking sandals and tennis shoes. That's when we realized we dug too deep. And still, they kept coming.

You had to laugh. Who could have expected this, from our beautiful sunny weather that morning?

"Welcome to the baby monsoon!" we joked.

Partygoers were packed, shoulder to shoulder, under the patio roof, as they ate. Soon, they escaped to the safety of the house, where a mud stain began from our bedroom (with a sliding glass door to the patio) to the wood floor of the formal living room and dining room. Pine needles (yet again) covered the floor, where people began packing their chairs as we opened presents and passed around cake.

There had to have been over fifty presents, from over fifty people. It was a beautiful disaster, absolute proof of how much we were loved, how much our baby was loved before she was even born. We had a mini pool tournament after, with our friends from my four pool teams. I took off my shoes, and we joked about how we would remember me playing pool barefoot and pregnant, not in the kitchen like other women.

I wondered what kind of omen the storm was for the baby to come.

The scream began somewhere deep in my gut, wrenching out of me like the child that would soon be pulled from my belly.

"Don't. Move." The anesthesiologist dug deep into my spine with the epidural needle, trying to find the right placement. We had already been through this once; he had placed it incorrectly, and as they began wheeling me to the operating room the first time, I told them I could still feel everything. We went back for another round. The doctor explained that he would have to try a different placement, which meant a larger chance for error. If I moved at all, I could end up paralyzed.

That's when the contractions began to turn, growing more intense and closer together. I watched the monitor show bigger, larger hills on the screen, while a nurse held me up by my left arm and my mother by my right, all of us bearing down and grunting in an effort to keep me still. Sweat and tears met on my cheeks, rolling down and off my chin. There was nowhere to hide from the pain, both from the contractions and the needle in my spine.

I don't remember falling asleep. I remember trying to wake, feeling light tugging on my belly, feeling the tube in my throat, and the lack of air.

I remember saying, "I can't breathe."

The doctor's reply: "If you can talk, you can breathe."

I remember lights, but my eyes were closed.

I remember her first cries, and that they tried to put her on my chest, but I pushed her away, saying, "I can't hold her." I was too drugged up; I was afraid I would drop her.

Logan held her for an hour, staring into her eyes while I slept.

When I woke, I tried to nurse, but she wouldn't latch and I didn't know what I was doing wrong. We didn't understand. A nurse put a binkie in her mouth, and she slept for twelve hours in a Mamaroo. We all slept so soundly. We had no idea how that first day would backfire.

A week later, we were rehospitalized with "Failure to thrive." Aurora came out at 11.5 pounds and lost more than two pounds from lack of nursing. She wasn't crying . . . she didn't know she was hungry, and neither did we.

Thus began the every-two-hour procedure of sleeping, nursing, pumping, washing, and sleeping again that I followed religiously, deliriously, for the first 6 months of Aurora's life. We discovered that when Aurora nursed, she wasn't suckling enough to get any milk, so Logan had to feed her with a tube of pumped milk attached to his finger. Once she got that down, we were able to graduate to nursing with a nipple shield, and then eventually to my bare breast, if I held it, and her, a very specific way. She nursed for forty-five minutes, I pumped for twenty, and then I washed and sanitized the pump components for ten. That left forty-five minutes to get some sleep, do a load of laundry, vacuum, and mop floors. Cry. Every. Single. Day.

It was grueling. It was heartbreaking, stressful. We fought. Logan had no idea what I was going through and didn't know how to help. But being in the trenches made us stronger. He learned how to put her to sleep on his own by bouncing her bouncer with his foot. He spent hours one day breaking her bottle strike so that I could start going back to pool again. One time, I drank too much and came home, saying I couldn't nurse and needed to sleep, so he got up and fed her and put her to bed. He learned her favorite lullabies and sang to her when he thought I couldn't hear.

And then he was gone.

Logan signed up for the military when Aurora was six months old, which meant he would be gone for basic training and advanced individual training (AIT) for six months shortly after she turned a year old.

I begged him not to do it, but one thing I've learned about my husband is that the harder you push, the harder he pushes back.

He was gone for six months, and while those months were hard, raising my first child alone, I also got to bond with her in a way that he didn't. She slept beside my bed in her pack and play crib; when she woke up at night, crying, I rolled over, reached in, and we both fell back asleep holding hands. In the morning, she would crawl into my bed and nurse, while I napped a little longer.

At that time, we lived on the same street as my grandparents and spent every single day taking long walks and then ending up at their house, for drinks or dinner, or both. My grandpa's health was diminishing, but he said that he lived for our visits. (After he passed, Grandma said she was certain Aurora kept him alive longer.)

As it has always done in our relationship, absence made the heart grow fonder. I had a little taste of what life might be like without Logan, and he, in return, missed me and Aurora. When he came back, he started the process of making it up to her (he still does, to this day). At first, she would have none of him, always reaching for mommy. He encouraged a binkie and the bottle, pushing me out the door to pool tournaments, league nights, and girls' nights out. Things were easier between them when I was gone, and I appreciated the break.

Soon enough, we fell into a stride as a family. But we both felt that something was missing . . . we agreed we wanted one more baby—well, I could have gone for three, but that wasn't in the cards. At least one more, so Aurora would have a companion. And we didn't want to wait too long; we wanted them to grow up close. We wanted her to have a little brother.

I was so sure this time. Of course we would have a boy. We already had a girl. Chances were better this one would be a boy. I didn't even save Aurora's old clothes, just in case. And when the nurse announced, "It's a girl!" once again, Logan cried while he laughed.

"No!" he demanded. "No. Not again."

And there went all his hopes of having a boy. Because my pregnancy was so high risk, they recommended I get my tubes tied while they were in there when the C-section was complete. We knew early on it would be another C-section when they saw that the placenta was growing over my cervix, blocking the baby's way out. If I went into labor, either the baby or I could bleed out. A third pregnancy would have raised the stakes even higher.

So we agreed. This was our last.

"You win," I said. "You got your two. I can't do another."

He nodded. "It's more important that you are alive."

He paused, head cocked to the side.

"If you think about it, we did have three. It's just that one is in heaven."

Heartwood

From the time you were a baby bump in my belly, Acacia, you've been molded around Aurora. I used to rock Aurora to sleep every night. I read her three or four books, sang three or four songs, nursed her, and then bounced or rocked her to sleep. Usually, she woke up when I laid her in her crib, so I had to hold her hand until she finally fell asleep. Many nights, she insisted on bouncing or rocking to sleep again . . . sometimes, for hours into the night. Aurora's bedtime routine was a struggle.

When you grew to the size of a cantaloupe inside me, Aurora started lying to the side of my belly. I inherited a La-Z-Boy rocking chair from my grandpa, and Aurora would sit on one of the huge stuffed arms, cuddled around my belly, sweet head in the crook of my neck or arm.

When you were a basketball, Aurora couldn't hug me. She couldn't get comfortable around us, and she kept falling off to the side of the chair. She was already angry and resentful of you, who had taken Aurora's place closest to my body. My milk dried up early on in my pregnancy—all of my body's energy and resources were diverted to the new baby.

There is a picture of Aurora in her crib at age two, having just woke up, hair a mess, looking confused and pissed off. We had jokingly printed a sign and put it on her crib, with a photo of the baby inside me, that read "EVICTION NOTICE: You have nine months to evacuate the premises." In another photo, Aurora has ripped the sign and photo off the crib and torn it in half.

I named you Acacia for the Persian tree, a hard wood said to have been used to build Noah's ark from the Bible story. Another word used for an acacia tree is "wattle," which may translate in Old Teutonic to mean "to weave." Wikipedia tells me that acacias are thought to have originally come from Australia and spread throughout the world from there. They are drought- and fire-resistant, growing in even the most untenable territory. Some species can be harvested for their seeds, which can be ground into flour or eaten raw or dried, with twenty-five percent more protein than common cereals. Acacias are a common food source for butterflies, and its bark and leaves have healing properties. Its sap is used in food and art supplies. Some species of acacia are poisonous.

Your middle name, Chante, means "heart" in Lakota. In ceremonies, I've heard that word, "chante" over and over, particularly in relation to "wacipi," which means "to dance." In my mind, "Acacia Chante" translates to the strong heartwood of an acacia tree. I picture acacia trees dancing in the wind in a desert, butterflies weaving in and out of their branches.

Your name was inspired from a night I was hospitalized because of false contractions. My pregnancy with you was high-risk; my placenta grew from the C-section scar where Aurora entered the world through my skin. It grew over my cervix, blocking your way out.

Placenta previa. That meant the doctors would have to take you out of my belly two months early, before I could start having contractions. Contractions from the cervix would put stress on my placenta, stretching it like thin dough until it broke. If the placenta tore, it would cause massive bleeding that could put us both in danger of dying.

I had to go in for monitoring twice a week to monitor both my vitals and yours and to check on your movement. Every time I went in, the nurses were astonished.

"Wow!" they exclaimed, looking at the screen of a monitor I couldn't see. "She's done a 360 in the ten minutes I've been gone."

"She's just kicking and kicking!"

"You have a little soccer player."

I wasn't at all surprised; I could feel you kicking my insides—my spine, my hips, my internal organs, my rib cage. All day, all night, the kicking.

The night I felt the contractions coming, I timed them like I was supposed to. I followed the 5-1-1 rule: Call the doctor when the contractions come every five minutes, lasting one minute each, for at least one hour. When I saw blood, I knew it was time to go in. It was still so early—a little over two months before your due date.

The hospital was eerily quiet at 2 a.m. Logan dozed in the waiting room while I dressed down for the examination. I fell asleep waiting on the cold, metal exam table in the middle of a big, dark room filled with monitors. It was like being on the set of a Star Trek episode, and the beeping and *husssshhhhh* of the machines made my eyelids heavy.

I felt cold hands and a gentle touch as the doctor took X-rays.

"Leah," he whispered. "I'm so sorry to wake you . . . but you have to see this." He turned the monitor around so I could see the screen.

A little green baby alien with a big head, small body, and wide eyes stared back at me. Next to your head, a raised, clenched fist.

"I just had to show you this," said the doctor. "I've never seen anything like this before. And it's so spooky, the way she is looking right at me . . . and how quiet and empty this room is . . . like she is going to fight me in the middle of the night."

"She's going to be a little fighter, a tough little girl."

I stared into your huge, wide eyes.

The contractions were deemed false labor. I felt silly for making Logan drive me to the hospital in the middle of the night, but I held that little nugget of knowing close to my chest: my baby would survive.

Aurora started singing and talking to you in the womb. She learned nursery rhymes at school and brought them home to sing to you. She sang the Native songs I sang to her her whole life. She laid her head on my belly and whispered secrets to her little sister that I couldn't hear.

I was raised with a little brother, my brother Ben, who I remember as always moving . . . running, skateboarding, riding his bike, BMXing, racing, snowboarding, hiking mountains. The only time he stays in one place is if he is stoned or drinking.

Because of Ben and my birth brothers, Sid and Levi, and the many boy cousins I grew up with, I am a tomboy at heart. Ben was the more gregarious of the two of us; I was always shy and quiet. He made friends, and I was the one who tagged along. When he started skateboarding, I got my own board and practiced ollies in our living room but was never as good as him or as brave. I dressed like a skater girl with baggy, torn-up jeans and a white tank, a red plaid button-down tied around my waist. I kissed the friends he had stay over at our house. One of his best friends, Jared, made me a ring out of a gum wrapper and asked me to marry him. As we grew older, every time I saw Jared, he blushed.

When we were maybe seven or eight, I had a crush on Ben's friend who lived across the street from us. I always dressed to fit in with the boys, and we didn't have a lot of money growing up, so my clothes were from the used bins at Goodwill, anyways. But I wanted to impress him, so one day I dressed in a white lace dress with a matching white hat and lace gloves. I walked across the street, which was unpaved with huge potholes we liked to play in when it rained, following my brother to go watch Ninja Turtles at Timmy's. Timmy was outside, calling to us to come over.

Ben ran into the house, and for a second, it was just me and Timmy outside, at the edge of the muddy street. Timmy was blushing, asking me why I was dressed "like that." I explained we had just come from church. His face kept getting redder, and suddenly, he pushed me backward, hands on my chest. Right into a muddy pothole.

I cried in the bath after, covered in mud. My dress was ruined. I stopped trying to look like a girl in front of the boys. I became really good at mimicking them.

As a teenager, I frequently found myself in spaces occupied by boys. I started tending fire for the men at the sweat lodge I went to. I wanted to be on the drum at powwows, not singing standing behind the guys I hung out with. I wanted to play basketball and soccer with the boys; I hated dance and volleyball.

When I went away to college, I joined a recreational basketball team. I had guy friends I went running with, played basketball with, went to the gym with. I grew up with my parents' pool table, so I was pretty decent at pool and could hold my own at the college bar. I called my mom up once in the middle of the night because a guy I liked was trying to tell me that I was wrong about a pool rule. He thought that if you hit a solid in and then scratch, then you still have to stick with solids. I called her to verify that the table is still considered open in that situation. She answered, voice heavy with sleep, and settled it—I was right—and laughed as she hung up on me.

There was always a boy who fell for me. I think because I was a girl and I was there and I loved the same things he loved, he thought that meant we were perfect for each other. I'd never chase after the boys I really liked. I let boys come to me, and then I'd give it a go, just because they made it easy. I never really loved any of them. Occasionally, I became infatuated with the way a guy would make me feel, but that wasn't love. The only boy I've ever fought for became my husband.

This time, when we found out the sex of the baby, Logan cried. Not in happiness—in fear. "*No!*" he exclaimed. He immediately started negotiating, as if he could talk his way out of it. "Is there a chance that you could be wrong? What is the percentage of error here?"

I laid back on the exam table and laughed, a deep, satisfying laugh. "Sisters." I whispered, in awe. I never thought of sisters.

I developed gestational diabetes again with the second pregnancy, but this time, we caught it earlier. Despite catching it early on, I couldn't control it on my own this time. I tried managing it through diet and exercise, as I had with Aurora's pregnancy. My blood sugar levels skyrocketed. I doubled down, restricting my carbs and exhausting myself with exercise. My doctor limited my exercise due to the placenta previa; my gestational diabetes doctors insisted I exercise more. I cried in frustration. Nothing worked and I was so hungry!

One doctor told me: "When you're hungry, just eat a bunch of vegetables." All I craved was carbs.

I had done this before. I knew what to do. I knew how to eat healthy; every lecture I got from the nutritionist defeated me. Finally, I gave in.

The insulin was a relief. I could finally eat again, and just a little insulin went a long way. I had to give myself shots twice a day, and we had to increase the insulin the longer the pregnancy went on. Logan winced every time I stuck a needle in my hip in front of him. I laughed. After a while, I didn't even feel it anymore.

After my pregnancy, it went away, but six months later, I tested high on my A1C. Prediabetic.

My own experience with sisters is fraught with negativity. I don't have a "real" sister . . . like one you were raised with your whole life and shares your DNA. But I have sisters.

1. Freya and Bernetta were my foster sisters when I was very young. I don't have any memories of Bernetta from that time because she ran away shortly after she came to live with us. Freya stayed for a little bit before she ran off. My only memory of Freya when we were kids is when she took me out on a floaty to the middle of a lake when we were camping and shoved me off. I was too young to swim, and I remember seeing water and sky, water and sky, as my head bobbed while I tried to stay afloat. I remember my mom picking me up off the shore.

   At my wedding, Freya was eight months pregnant and brought her stripper friend *and* her boyfriend as her plus one and got completely wasted while her friend gave my grandpa a lap dance and the boyfriend stole bottles of alcohol. My caterer tackled her and took her keys when she tried to get in the van and drive her children home drunk.

When I was pregnant with Aurora, I told Freya at a family gathering, and she yelled "No you're not!" and flung a glass of water in my face.

2. Bethany was a year old when they brought her, moving her in the middle of the night while she slept. She was too young to have night terrors. There is a picture of me and Bethany and Ben on a slide at the park. My mom was trying to adopt her when her aunt came and claimed her for the government checks. They moved her in the middle of the night again. My mom cried, broken hearted, for years after. She still does.

3. When I found out I had a birth sister two years older than me, I couldn't wait to meet her. We both had black widow tattoos we got before we knew about each other; we both forgot to fill in the poisonous red on the back and planned to do so together. We went by the same street name as teenagers: Pixie. My niece thought I was her doppelganger, and I confused photos of the two of us, thinking her photos were of me at first glance. Petra broke my heart and hers, repeatedly, choosing meth over us both. Now, she's sober, and I still can't bring myself to trust her. She's been sober before.

4. Bernetta came back once. She stayed at Freya's. I came over for dinner, and we talked and laughed. It felt like she could really be like an older sister. I've never seen her again.

5. When my adoptive mom's birth daughter found her, my mom took me out on the porch and showed me the letter Paige sent. Her handwriting was just like my mom's. I was truly happy for her. I had just found my birth mother and birth siblings, and I knew that was hard for my adoptive family. Now we were even.

   When I met Paige, she told me she wasn't trying to replace me. I felt like I had taken her spot. I tried to move over for her, make space for her. I was excited to have a sister.

She was mean to her husband, Shawn. She flirted with other men and held it over his head. She talked down to him, bossing him around.

She laughed just like my mom, looked just like her. She bought my mom a ring and sat next to her every chance she got. She even squeezed her chair between us if we sat together. When she got jealous, she flirted with my boyfriend.

After years of her behavior, I decided it was war, and I wasn't going to let her win. I started flirting with her husband, who blossomed at the attention, showing me his photography. Paige moved her seat back to her husband, and I went and sat next to my mom again.

She asked me what I wanted for my wedding, how she could help. I told her I needed blue high heels. She bought me cheap white flip flops that were too small for me. My heel hung off the back. I was going to wear them anyways, but my bridesmaids hid them from me.

During the wedding photos, Logan asked for a photo with "just the family he knows . . ." meaning without Paige and Shawn. (He didn't intend to hurt anyone; he is not the best with words. And now I am so thankful to him because we have wedding photos without them.) Paige cried and told everyone I asked for her to not be in the photos. My aunt Peggy gave me a present that Paige thought was hers (it was the same spice rack), and Paige cried to my family that I would not recognize the gift as hers. She left, refusing to talk or say goodbye.

Years later, I saw her at a family reunion. I said "Hi, Paige," and she ignored me. My aunt Dayna came behind me and announced, "I saw that."

I tried making amends via Facebook Messenger multiple times. I tried calling her out in front of family I heard she was shit-talking to. It's been ten years.

Last year, I sent her a long message about how we are family, sisters, and how I would welcome dropping it all and starting over again.

Her response: "I'm ok with letting the past be the past."

I screamed as I heard a *plop!* of my own blood hit the floor.

"It's not working!" I yelled at the anesthesiologist; my face squeezed up in pain. "I can feel everything!"

He looked down at something, some mechanism that was supposed to gauge my pain and was, yet, clearly failing.

"Do you want to be awake to see your baby, or are you okay if you fall asleep?"

It was my own fault. I told them not to give me too much pain medication this time around. Last time, I was so zonked out, I missed Aurora's first hour of life.

I hesitated in my response. Was I being a wimp? I am not really a wimp. I have a high pain tolerance. Women with lower pain thresholds told me that you aren't supposed to feel anything with a C-section. Why did this hurt so much? How come I could feel the knife?

They gave me more local anesthesia, knocked up the pain medication a tick more. I could still feel things, sharp things, but I wanted to see you. I wanted that blissful moment when they gave you to me and I held you on my chest.

When they pulled you out of me and had Logan cut the cord, they let him bring you to my face so I could see you. I was preoccupied with the pain from every stitch, watching the heads of the five doctors surrounding me over the barrier set up so I couldn't see my own insides.

"Leah, look," said Logan, smiling, looking down at the baby. He was trying to distract me.

It worked for a minute. I stopped crying and yelling long enough to look up at you. Your face was a blur through my tears. You didn't look like the alien baby I saw on that 2 a.m. monitor. You were so much tinier than Aurora. I hoped we would be able to keep you out of the NICU. You were so little.

When I was sewn up, they moved me to an interim room while they monitored my vitals post-surgery. Logan came to set you on my chest.

We had a plan. We had seen all of the videos the hospital shows you to prepare you for this moment. The plan was that he would set you on my chest, and we would let you find your own food source. I really wanted to see that happen. With Aurora, I was passed out from the pain medication, so I wasn't able to hold her. She kept rolling when they set her on me, so Logan just held her until I woke up. She wasn't interested in nursing that whole first day. She just stared into her daddy's eyes.

I remember getting into the car with Aurora the first time, Logan driving us home. I burst into tears, and then started laughing hysterically.

"They are just going to let us walk out of here with her?" I wailed, wiping my face. "We don't know what the fuck we are doing."

Logan, surprised, looked over at me with wide eyes. "I know, right?" He laughed with me.

I looked back at her over my shoulder.

"I mean, how are we supposed to keep this tiny human alive? We can barely keep ourselves alive."

Nursing Aurora was difficult. Neither of us knew what we were doing. We had to receive in-hospital coaching and supervision before they would release me with my daughter, and then we spent three months using a nipple shield and a C-clamp to help her get the right suction. I had to hold her with one hand and then hold my breast in just the right position with the other for Aurora to be able to nurse. She cried and screamed if I took my hand away to shake it awake or reach for something—my water, the remote, my cell phone, a book.

Acacia, you were born knowing exactly what you want and insisting on it. As Logan brought your naked body closer to my bare chest, you craned your tiny, brand-new neck, and your whole body pushed against him, guiding him to my nipple. You knew exactly where you needed to go, and you latched on your own, without needed any support or help or guidance. It was like magic. The anticipation of the months of stress and agony and frustration Aurora and I experienced disappeared just like that—*poof!* This time, it would be different. I relaxed.

In fact, I fell asleep. Every time you nursed, a rush of hormones went straight to my brain, mingled with the oxytocin from the IV drip, and made me fall asleep. And you fed often. I fell asleep mid-sentence, talking to my parents. When my grandma and aunt came, I remember trying so hard to keep my head up, but it kept falling forward. I had lots of nice, discreet nursing tops, which was a good investment, because you wanted to nurse constantly. So I slept a lot. I found ways of propping you up with a pillow so I wouldn't lay on your face, and Logan kept an eye on you, picking you up when you were through and putting you to sleep in the little plastic box they put next to my bed. He remembered swaddling and the five *S*'s we were taught in our "What to expect" classes when I was pregnant with Aurora. We had it down this time.

Still, I asked to stay an extra day. We probably didn't need it, but Logan' military insurance was paying for everything, and I knew that if we went home, I would need to take care of everyone. As long as we were in the hospital, everyone took care of me.

My mom only stayed at grandma's house down the street for a few days this time to help me after I got out of the hospital. She was working a lot. Logan and I knew what we were doing. You and I mostly slept together, nursing and cuddling.

Aurora was told to leave us alone, let us rest. Aurora and I had been attached from the beginning; I wore her in a carrier until long into toddlerhood. Being separated from me in favor of her sister was devastating for Aurora.

And yet, she loved her new little sister more passionately than she resented you. There is a photo of Aurora's face when she first saw and held you—pure joy. I have videos of Aurora singing to you and cuddling you in bed, hugging you and talking to you and singing to you and laughing.

Up until she turned four, Aurora introduced you to people as her baby. "This is Acacia. She is *my* baby!" she would say, trying to pick up your car seat in the crook of her arm, like me. If someone tried to get close to look at you, Aurora would step in between, telling them "No! This is *my* baby!"

Even now, at age five, Aurora speaks for you, telling us what you need and want. You are almost three and don't talk half as much as Aurora did at age three because you don't have to—Aurora speaks for you. But Aurora is about to go to kindergarten and you are going to have to start using your own voice.

Grandpa is in the Garden

My grandpa is in the hydrangea bush that grows in front of my grandma's house. He makes the flowers turn amazing colors—green to blue to purple to a pink-red, sometimes all at once—all seasons of the year. I have a bouquet of flowering branches from the bush that my aunt brought me over a month ago that are still going strong in my windowsill.

Before he died, the bush never flowered. Despite his green thumb, it resisted his prodding. No matter how much he watered or touched or talked to it, it would not produce. Every year—sometimes multiple times a year—I heard him declare that he was just going to cut it down, but he never did.

The year before he died, as he grew more frail and went outside less and less, he told us that if that bush flowered after he died, we should all know that it was him. He died in the early spring, and within weeks, it flowered. We all cried when we saw the first tender green petals. (I couldn't make this up if I tried.)

When he died, I felt him everywhere. I stayed up all night, sleeping in his favorite chair in the kitchen, using his lavender heating pad, reheating it in the microwave again and again, smelling his scent again every time the pad heated up. I got up early and went to the store to get the makings for stew. I made so much stew, way more than we could eat. I didn't want anyone to have to think about or worry about food or feeding anyone when they were mourning.

As I was picking the rosemary and thyme and basil from his garden to make the stew, I suddenly felt him all around me. I stopped picking and lifted my head, smelling the air. The fresh morning breeze smelled like him. I could feel the sudden heaviness of his presence all around me. My eyes prickled with tears, and my breath caught in my chest.

My aunt came up behind me when I was stirring the stew.

"Mmmm! That smells so good!" she exclaimed, smiling despite her red-rimmed eyes.

I turned to her slightly, in all seriousness, and responded, "Grandpa is in the stew. He is in the rosemary, and the thyme, and the basil. He's in the garden."

She hesitated, searching my eyes.

"Well then. I'll have to go see him." She went outside to talk to her dad.

My grandparents met very young, when Grandpa was serving in the military. Grandma remembers waiting for him to get back from overseas, living in an apartment in San Francisco with roommates. Other than her father's house and her home with my grandpa, that's the only other home she had ever known. She hated living with roommates.

For their fiftieth wedding anniversary, someone had copied old photos of them when they were young and pasted them on cardboard displays, set up on foldable tables as we walked into the banquet room at the University Hotel in Portland, where my aunt worked.

"Wow! Grandma was hot!" I exclaimed over a photo of grandma on the beach in a black one-piece bathing suit with cutouts. "I didn't even know they had those types of swimsuits back then."

There were photos of them in their twenties, Grandma with curls and Grandpa with the same smirky smile fifty years later. They were in love, Grandma's head tilted slightly toward him, his eyes glittering with the lights reflected in them. Photo after photo just showed proof of their love and their commitment to each other and their family.

When Logan and I were engaged, Grandma drank too much wine and told me that I had two options. I could fall in love with my husband and then fall out of love with my husband, divorce him, and then fall in love with someone else, or I could choose to fall in and out of love with my husband again and again. She had chosen the second option, obviously.

"You always have that choice," she said, pointing her wrinkled finger for emphasis, "because you won't always be in love with each other, and you need to know and expect that." It was one of the wisest things she told me.

Grandpa told us that "Yes, dear" really means "Fuck you." I can still hear the exact pitch of his voice and see his infamous accompanying eye roll when he said that, and Grandma's quick *look* across the room that made it clear that she knew *exactly* what he meant.

Your great grandpa Schröder's eye rolls were the best. One of my favorite Grandpa-isms. That and "*Every damn time!*" as he smacked his hand down on the table after *yet another* glass of wine spilled or dropped to the floor during dinner. Once during Thanksgiving, someone knocked a glass over on the white tablecloth, the burgundy spilling out over the serving plates so neatly plated and set.

A dramatic pause before we all slammed our hands down on the table, all twenty-five of us, as one:

"*Every* ***damn*** *time*!"

And then peals of laughter. Rolling, unrestrainable laughter—from Grandpa most of all, tears rolling down his face.

Now that I finally have a home big enough for entertaining thirty people, and Grandma is selling her house, we've officially been asked to take over the annual family Christmas Eve party. On the one hand, it is a high honor to be asked to host an event so important—everyone looks forward to this party every year. On the other hand . . . *damn them!* This is going to mean weeks of cleaning and organizing and decorating and cooking and preparing. Weeks of stress and demands and drama. Weeks of arguments between Logan and I over all of the above, likely. And then weeks of cleaning and apologizing and forgiving and discussing afterwards. I am both dreading and looking forward to it.

Logan is absolutely ecstatic—he *loves* Christmas. He loves everything about it. The music, the weather, the family, the presents, the food. But most of all—the decorations.

It is October and a quarter of our garage is already filled with Christmas decorations. Logan won't let me store the girls' summer clothes in the garage, but a hundred holiday baubles is fine. Twenty garlands and seven Christmas decorative pillows is just fine, too. He wants us to go to a warehouse sale for lighting equipment . . . not just string lights, lighting equipment . . . despite the four large light-up lawn ornaments and traditional cheap string lights we have already.

In fact, he's so excited about Christmas, he's gotten out of control with Halloween. He bought candy and zombie-themed bowls to hold the candy in September. He bought five pumpkins and carving supplies and banners to go on the side of the house that say "It's October, witches!" and "Boo!" He bought a scary clown that hangs on the front door. When you push a button on his nose, it laughs hysterically and shakes, knocking its hard head and skeleton legs against the door. My daughters, ages three and five, run past the door when they need to get in and out. My youngest calls him "Boo" and cries when he laughs and shakes.

Just yesterday, Logan came home with a look like his tail was between his legs.

"I did it again," he mumbled, eyes downcast and scuffing his feet on the floor, holding a gigantic box in his arms.

I gave him a *look*.

"What now?"

He moved his left arm so I could see the picture of a blow-up lawn ornament, a tacky white ghost holding a carved pumpkin. The ghost lights up and there is an automatic blower that airs it up, like the fancy air mattress we use for guests. It's over six feet tall.

It's only three days until Halloween. It's not like we are going to get a lot of use out of it this year. He has an addiction.

While Logan stockpiles décor, I prepare myself emotionally. All the memories come welling up in my mind, some of the warmest, happiest days of my childhood. Grandpa's Christmas decorations, the warm glow of the twinkling lights wrapped around the tree in the living room, with what seemed like hundreds of presents stacked around it, bows and tinsel and glitter. And the food—so much food! Early on in my youth, there was a full dinner, with Christmas ham and gravy and sweet potatoes drenched in melted marshmallows.

That was before we started inviting more extended family, and then their closest friends. For a few years, there was only standing room, and the house got so hot that everyone stripped down to their tank tops underneath their ugly Christmas sweaters. Eggnog-fueled fights broke out over the White Elephant game. (Ever since then, we've had to post the rules for the White Elephant event on Facebook weeks in advance.) We stopped having a full dinner, and we removed the liquor from the tables (those in the know kept a stash in Grandma's bedroom). It was only beer and wine for a long while, and the food was reduced to hors d'oeuvres.

That is when we fell in love with my uncle Kevin's cheese dip. He is from Texas, and his cheese dip included Velveeta and meat, veggies, and spices. He always brought a huge crockpot and an extra-large bag of chips. I don't ever remember there being leftover cheese dip.

This year, they will all come out to our new house in the country. I'm not sure where everyone will stay. It won't be the same when we can't all just walk down the street, tipsy and arms linked to help each other across the ice to our own houses. It won't be the same without my uncle's cheese dip. It won't be the same without Grandpa.

Every year, Grandpa made homemade coffee liquor and gave out bottles as presents. In honor of him, this year, Logan and I are making our own homemade coffee liquor, complete with moonshine rum made in a still on our back porch. We are commissioning a friend to make a label for the liquor. We are calling it "Prost!" which means "Cheers!" in German, and it's going to include a short description honoring Grandpa. We are going to hand out bottles to each couple and tell them we want the spirit of Grandpa to be with us this year

There was a tree in the middle of your great-grandparents' house when you were little, Aurora.

No, not a Christmas tree. I am no longer talking about Christmas. I'm talking about a pine tree. A huge, centuries-old pine tree, right smack in the middle of Grandma's house.

The house used to be much smaller, see. I remember it having more walls when I was a little girl. They knocked down a bunch of the walls and expanded it, and when they expanded it, they debated about what to do about that tree.

Grandpa didn't have the heart to cut it down, so he decided to build around it.

The tree is a focal point of the house. When people walk through, they lose their minds.

"There is a *tree* in the middle of this house!" they exclaim in wonder.

"Oh, yeah," we say. "There is." As if we've never considered it. Because, well . . . we haven't. We grew up with it this way. It's been this way for twenty, thirty years.

Sometimes, though, if we're bored or feel like impressing someone, we will take them on a tour to show them the tree at Grandma's house. As a teenager, I delighted in giving these tours on the way to the pool in my grandparents' backyard, watching the looks of surprise on the faces of my friends when they turned the corner from the living room to the family room and saw the tree.

I remember when Grandpa decided he needed a moat around the tree. I think there was an actual logistical purpose for it, but when I was a kid, it was just a really cool water feature. I loved plugging in the electrical cord, which triggered a waterfall to dribble out of the wall, down a cascade of river rocks Grandpa had fashioned, filling up the moat surrounding the bottom of the tree. After a few years of use, it wouldn't work anymore, so he just filled the moat with smaller rocks. During the holiday season, Aunt Dayna filled the moat with twinkling lights and tulle (sans water).

The tree also posed several problems, primarily with the roof surrounding it. When the wind blew, the tree pushed against the roof, causing it to crack around the edges. The ceiling started falling down around the tree. Grandpa and Uncle Mark had to patch it regularly and do some major work every few years or so. There is also the matter of the roots.

I'm with Grandma at the beach. She's staying here while the house is being shown. The two of you and I are the first ones to visit her.

Logan has a military drill weekend, so I decided to take the girls to see Grandma. It's the first weekend she will be spending at the beach after moving everything out of the house she's lived in for the past fifty years. At age ninety, she's gone through half a century's worth of her belongings, without my grandpa, and moved out of her house. She says she's relieved.

She does seem lighter, happier. Her color seems more flushed, and she moves more sprightly than she has the past two years since he passed. She offers me a glass of wine after I bring everything in from the car in the middle of a coastal rainstorm. The pack and play, the bedding, the clothes and shoes for one woman and two little girls, the toys so they have something to do, the books for bedtime, the sound machine, toiletries, raincoats, hoodies, diapers. Even when everything is brought in and set up and laid out and put away, I have trouble sitting down. A mother never stops moving. I feel the urge to move everything breakable in the little beach house to somewhere safe, out of my toddler's reach.

Grandma retires early. My girls wear her out. They've worn me out, frankly. I've had a couple glasses of wine, read my book, and I am ready to sleep. But they aren't. Aurora keeps rolling around in her sleeping bag, excited by the new environment. My girls have their own rooms at home, so they are unused to being in the same room with each other at nighttime. They delight in making little noises at each other while they play in their beds. The little noises soon become big noises, and next I know, they are screaming happily, manically, across the room.

It's after midnight and this tired mama has had enough. I yell at them both to quiet down, it's nighttime. They laugh at me, silly mama. I put them each in time out in the bathroom, one at a time, just to get some quiet, just for a minute each. Just long enough for them to know I am serious. It works. Rora eventually stops rolling around. Cacia goes right to sleep; I've never put her in time out. I feel guilty, but it's worth it because it is quiet, and I can finally sleep.

No one tells you how little you will sleep when you are a mother. No one tells you how crazy it will make you feel. No one tells you how it will take you to the edge and back.

The next day, we get up slowly, lazily. I make Grandma breakfast—eggs with goat cheese and pumpkin rolls. The girls never get cinnamon rolls, and these ones are pumpkin, to boot. They shovel the large rolls in their mouths greedily, barely stopping to get a breath in, afraid this is too good to be true.

Grandma eats like a bird, has always eaten like a bird, but she's satisfied. I'm not a fan of instant coffee, but hers is magic somehow. I remember Grandpa used to get this brand—Taster's Choice. They would always store it in a fancy container, so it seemed fancier than regular instant coffee.

We talk, and we also sit in silence. I love that we can talk about deep things, shallow things, happy things, sad things, and then we can also say nothing at all, and it all feels like the same thing.

We take the girls to the beach, stopping at my favorite little bead shop on the way. Grandma gets winded easily, so she sits on a log near the car while we walk down to the water. The girls can't help themselves, as I knew they would. They start by daintily dipping their toes in the water, but it isn't long before they are tumbling in the waves. I pull them out and take them to where Grandma is sitting. They play in the sand, and when they are somewhat dry, I change them into warm clothes. Rora makes a game of picking sea grass and then "replanting" it all in one spot.

Grandma watches them, soaking it all in, as I knew she would. This is why I do it, all of it, even though it's so hard . . . schlepping the kids and all of our things all over the place, less-than-ideal sleeping arrangements for such young children, the lack of sleep.

She told me once after Grandpa died that she thinks he stayed alive so long because I brought Aurora to see him almost every day. I want her to stay young, too.

When the girls get warm in their car seats, they both fall asleep. Grandma and I get cans of wine from the store and sit in the car, drinking our wine and chatting as the sun sets.

This, too, I think, as I soak in the warmth from the setting sun and watch a family playing with a kite, listening to Grandma tell stories, and then sitting in silence.

Grandma is sitting in my dining room. Her realtor is perched across from her, on the edge of his seat, back straight. There are piles of papers between them.

She called me the night before, saying, "My realtor and I will be at your house tomorrow at 11 a.m. to sign some papers." She said it so casually that it didn't sink in until later that she had sold her home.

They both are wearing face masks, in the midst of the COVID pandemic. Because we live in a rural county with very low COVID cases, we don't usually think about wearing face masks unless we are walking into a store or place of business, let alone our own home, so the masks at my dining table startle me.

When the realtor leaves, Grandma sighs.

"$420,000," she breathes heavily, leaning back, the tension visibly leaving her body. Now she can get started on having her new home built, one that will be all hers. She's picked a plot on my parents' property in Quilcene, Washington, in the Olympic National Forest, right on the peninsula, right next to a large, wild creek that is lately more like a river as the ice caps melt. She will be able to walk to the water to watch the salmon spawn, to wake up and see a herd of elk out her window. She will also be steps away from my mother, who is a nurse and will be able to take care of her as she grows older.

The last night she stayed in her house, the night before she left for the beach house, I got a call at around 5 p.m. I was on the beach with my brother, Ben, and my friends and their kids. We had spent a few hours during the last river-worthy day of the year, playing in the sand and the water, kayaking in the waves, and watching the kids swim. We had just made a fire and roasted hot dogs, and we were all getting chilly in the cooling wind. We could feel the very last rays of summer leaving the earth in that moment.

I answered, and it was Aunt Dayna.

"It's Grandma's last night at the house," she spoke roughly, "And I just wanted you to know we are making one last fire in the backyard for her. I wouldn't want you to miss it."

Ben and I didn't even think twice about going. We packed up the girls and kayaks, said our goodbyes, and dropped the girls and gear off with Logan back at the house on our way to Portland.

Remember that little tree that used to be at the side of the house, that Grandpa cut down when he realized we were all using it to climb over the fence to get to the pool to go skinny-dipping in the middle of the night? I used to sneak up there to read and listen in on people's conversations in the driveway for hours.

Remember when they had a hot tub in the back room, and how it smelled like chlorine super strong, and how we would get out and jump into the pool and then go back and forth for hours, how your body froze up when you'd hit the cold water, and how much we loved that feeling?

Remember we used to float on our backs at night and look up at the stars?

Remember Levi kissed me under the water, how people acted like they didn't know, but there used to be an underwater light, so you could actually see everything.

Remember there was a Ouija board that Freya used one time, and she was watching a scary movie, and Grandma said she saw the paper airplanes on the ceiling start spinning? She took away the Ouija board and locked it up in the newalls—an old word my grandma used for the storage space in a house's walls—in the upstairs room where Abbie was staying, and it was there for years. Everyone who has stayed in that room has had bad dreams, except Abbie, because they found it and threw it away right before Grandpa passed, before Abbie moved in.

When we walk through the house to the backyard, Grandma is already a bottle deep, the wine buzz making her throat guttural. She squeezes us tight, telling us it made her night we came. Ben rarely shows for family events, as he is usually working or not in town, but he wanted to be there that night as much as I did. It was about saying goodbye to our youth, goodbye to Grandpa.

My cousins, Allie and Abbie, and my aunts are there, too, and we toast to the house, to Grandpa, to Grandma, to the pool—to all the memories. We use all the rest of the pile of wood, the pile that has always been plentiful, never empty.

When we leave, I cry softly so Grandma can't hear me, realizing this is the last time I will walk across this grass in this backyard, barefoot and buzzed under the stars, warm from the fire and the whiskey. This is the last time I will walk through this kitchen, where my grandma and my aunts and my mother and my cousins have made countless meals, had countless important discussions, shared countless secrets. This is the last time I will use this bathroom, see my reflection in these mirrors, next to the bathtub I have given my babies countless baths in. This is the last time I will walk through this dining room, where we have shared so many family meals, hosted annual Christmas Eve parties, fought, and loved.

On the night of our wedding, Logan and I snuck into this room to peek into the pile of gifts left for us to open the next day, giggling like children.

I've fallen asleep, pregnant, on this couch so many times. This chair has rocked both of my babies to sleep, night after night. This is the last time that I will be opening this door, one of the many times this door opens in a day with family members passing back and forth through it, proving how loved my grandparents are/were.

I give the hydrangeas outside the door a kiss as I pass by on my way to the car.

Dead Deer Highway

My birth father once told me that the best thing he'd ever done for me was to let me go so that I would never know anything about our reservation. He was right.

The road in front of me seems to disappear into a pitch-black hole in the sky. The night is so dark, my headlights are like a flashlight sputtering before it is about to go out.

On my car speakers, a thriller podcast about a serial killer who abducts young girls and leaves them to die alongside a highway in the middle of nowhere parallels the dark countryside around me.

And then, the bodies.

The first one I see barely at the corner of my right eye. It is a quick flash of meat at the side of the road, there and gone so quickly I believe it when I tell myself it's just a large boulder.

But then there are more, closer to the road so that I can make out their shapes. Short brown hair, soft white tufts under long ears . . . I imagine them silky to the touch. Hoofs splayed out at strange angles. I pass semis that I believe could barrel through deer barely even registering the impact and understand how this happens.

Dead Deer Highway, I start calling it in my mind.

Then, there is the construction, changing traffic routes and throwing barricades in my path. A concrete wall juts out into the road at one point, and the car in front of me swerves quickly to miss it.

I follow, glad for the short, yet perceptible warning. My husband, Logan, stirs, sleeping in the seat beside me.

I arrive at a gas station near Goble, Utah, which is just outside of Salt Lake City, shaken and breathless. I ask a trucker I see standing just inside the station store if it gets any better.

"What, the road?" *Yes*. "Oh, you mean the deer and the construction?" *Yes*. "You're almost to the city. You'll be alright from there. I do this leg every day, back and forth for fifteen hours." I thank him and fill another Styrofoam cup of coffee.

We make it to Salt Lake in one piece. I wake up Logan at 4 a.m. Mountain Standard Time and tell him he has to drive. I've driven fifteen hours at that point. I've had six cups of coffee. I'm shaking from the adrenaline and caffeine, and the road has been wavy for a while now.

My eyelids are heavy, but I can't sleep when he takes over. For one thing, he blares Mongolian war music to stay awake. For another, we just hit the Rockies. Between the two, plus the caffeine, I feel like we are flying through the night on our path to death. The thriller podcasts and Dead Deer Highway are still fresh in my mind.

I keep laying down, with my seat all the way back, and then jumping up every time we hit a bump or take a quick swerve around a corner. Logan tells me to knock it off and go to sleep, but I can't. He says I remind him of a meerkat, popping up and down again. He pushes my chest back so I lay down. He tells me everything is okay.

I finally let go, realizing that if we have an accident, I have a higher likelihood of surviving if my muscles are relaxed while sleeping. And I'm going to have to drive again when Logan gets tired.

I drift off to the sounds of whooping men and growling and bass.

Funeral arrangements for Edwin Francis Blackfeather, age 69 of Lake Park, IA, are pending with the Sioux Funeral Home of Pine Ridge, SD. Edwin made his journey to the Spirit World on August 27, 2020 at the Pearl Valley Rehabilitation Center in Lake Park, IA.

Two days earlier:

Facebook just told me that my birth father died. The concept is both ironic and fitting. I re-read the announcement of my birth father's death on the Pine Ridge Funeral Home's Facebook page. *Yes, that's him.*

I'm stunned—more so because he was still alive, and I hadn't heard from him. I would have been less surprised if he had been dead for a long time and no one knew. I haven't heard from him in years. He used to have my cell phone number memorized, and he called me every six months to a year whenever he was detoxing or in prison.

"Baby girl," he called me, because that's what was on my birth certificate when they knew I wouldn't be with them long enough to have a name. My birth sister, Petra, likes to remind me that she and Sid are the only ones that share our birth father's last name, as if that somehow makes them more connected, despite the fact that she never spoke to him again after he left them when they were very young. For years, I begged her to call him; I was so afraid she would regret it if he died and she never heard his voice again.

At least I know where he is now.

I am antsy, a jangle of too-raw nerve endings. I have so much to do before we leave for the funeral; I have nothing to do. I need to get out, away. Something in me is awake, anxious, raw, wild . . . not like a mother or a wife or a dependable daughter or coworker, all the things I've come to associate with myself. I feel an edge. Something dangerous. Something that needs to hunt.

I escape to a river beach down the Columbia near Rainer, eighteen miles from where we moved recently in St. Helens, Oregon. I drive far enough that I don't recognize where I am. I drive to a wide-open space blasting cold, cleansing wind off the river. I sit in a folding chair I keep in my car in case I find myself out in nature. I don a warm hoodie I keep for cold moments in my trunk. I feel a strong urge to drink whiskey until I'm warm. But I don't have any whiskey. I let the wind blow through me, and I empty my body of tears. (That's the last time I'll cry until I bury him.)

I tell the water to take my words to him.

I tell him I love him, even though he wasn't there. I tell him I know he wanted to be.

I tell him about his granddaughters.

I sing him peyote songs.

I tell him I will remember him.

I tell him I forgive him.

The water gives me back a light green clam shell, deposited at my feet. All the others are gray and white. I pick it up and hold it in my pocket. I put it in a little compartment in my car where I can keep an eye on it. Maybe one day I'll put it on a necklace and keep it close to my heart.

I don't imagine I will ever receive any of his belongings. I don't know that he had any belongings. They said he was in detox when the police guards beat him, when he fell and hit his head, when he slipped into a coma. He was in a coma for four months, and no one thought to contact his children. He died before I could say goodbye. Maybe he was going to use his only phone call to call me that night.

I keep thinking, *At least now I know.*

I get a call from a 605 area code. It's Mike, the funeral director, with Aunt Bree and Aunt Maureen on speakerphone. Mike conferences in Petra and proceeds to ask a series of questions.

"Do you want to do a wake?" *Yes.*

"When can Leah and Petra be here to attend the wake?" *Thursday.*

"What time would work?" *Afternoon. 3–5pm.*

"When do you want to do the funeral and burial the next morning?" *10 a.m. start.*

Then, the harder questions.

"When was his birthday?" *October 18, 1950. (Petra and I didn't know the answer.)*

"Are there any other children besides Petra, Sid, Leah, and Levi?" *We think so, but don't know for sure. He said he had two children after us, two girls who would be in their twenties now, but we don't know anything about them.*

"How many family members have passed?" *Too many.* "What are their names?" *We almost forget to include Dayton, Levi's baby who passed away at eight months old from Sudden Infant Death Syndrome, right before I met Levi.* Aunt Maureen has a long list of names.

We finalize the details for the pamphlets. The wake would be at Aunt Maureen's daughter Trisha's house, one street away from the funeral home. Due to COVID, the tribe would provide a tipi that would need to be set up in the yard, and the funeral home would deliver the body to the tipi. People would come and visit our father's body in the tipi throughout the night.

My nephew's head is soft and silky and smells like brown sugar and baby powder. I wonder at how intoxicating babies smell after you've had your own and they aren't babies anymore.

I dance him around the Denny's where we meet Petra and my Aunt Jilah, who is dropping off Petra and then continuing on to see her friends in Wyoming.

Their eyes and questions are assessing, probing. They tell me I look good after losing all my baby weight. Petra complains that hers is stubborn. I tell her it took me almost two years after Acacia was born before the pounds started melting off, and then it happened quickly. Not being able to drink so much while nursing helped. Cacia, at two, is almost weaned, and I both hope and fear that she will forget about nursing when I come back.

When we buckle Jordan in his car seat, which we switched to my car from Aunt Jilah's, he protests loudly for about five minutes. That's the last time we hear him really cry during the whole trip. We ask Petra how she ended up with The Best Baby Ever. He sleeps the six hours to Rapid City, almost the whole way.

We plan on sharing a hotel room with two queens for the two nights we will be there. There is no hotel on the reservation, so this is as close as we are going to get. We will do some sightseeing and see our brother Levi's family while we are there, do a little shopping for fun. These detours will give us a break from the intensity of the wake and burial.

Petra and I coax Logan into watching the baby after dinner so we can go check out the hot tub and pool. No one else is in the spa room, so we get it all to ourselves.

"We should get some alcohol and get drunk," says Petra. She's in recovery from meth. When she's in town, she has to take UAs daily from her probation officer when she's in town. But she's not in town right now, so no one would know. She received a special reprieve to attend her father's funeral.

I tell her everything is closed or closing and I'd rather spend time at the pool. She tells me I'm no fun anymore. I tell her parenting has made me responsible . . . and tired.

Suddenly, she's no longer interested in the pool. I swim laps while she yells into her phone at her boyfriend, Derek, who is in prison. I can't tell why they are fighting. He seems to be trying to placate her. She won't stop yelling and swearing.

"Are you going to swim?" I ask her. She looks at me and raises one finger while berating poor Derek. I throw up my hands and walk over to the hot tub.

She hangs up on Derek, then tells me he is an idiot. We check out the sauna for a few minutes, but it's not very warm. Her phone rings.

"Hey, baby?" she answers. Now they are telling each other they love each other and cooing at each other. I tell her I'm heading back upstairs to the room. Logan and I watch movies on our tablets until she comes back up, slipping in bed next to The Sleepiest Baby Ever, who barely moves as she adjusts the pillows and leans back, sober and sighing.

There is a barricade up at the reservation border and an electronic sign that tells us it's a COVID checkpoint. We don our face masks as a volunteer walks up to the car with a clipboard.

"Reason for visiting?" comes a gruff voice through the mask. He has his pen raised.

"Our father's funeral."

"Name?"

"Mine or his?"

"His."

"Edwin Blackfeather."

"Name?"

"Mine?"

"Yes."

"Leah Altman."

Petra rolls down her window in the back.

"Petra Blackfeather." I look back at her, my left eyebrow raised. *Really?* As if her name makes her anymore his daughter than me. She never even wanted to know him until he died.

"Fine. Roll through."

We continue on.

Five minutes down the road, I get pulled over. The reservation cop tells me we were going eighty. We were going sixty-five—the speed limit—but I know better than to argue. I visit the rez once every ten years. I'm not worried about having to pay the fine. Just worried we are going to be late.

The funeral home is quiet and homey, with old couches that remind me of someone's grandma's house. We wait and wait for our family. They are late putting up the tipi.

Logan and I leave Petra, against her wishes, with Jordan at the funeral home to drop off some food we brought for the wake. We've been warned about my Aunt Trisha's. The people who live there or visit often are well-known drug addicts. Bad things happen there. We don't know details, but we know we need to be careful. We plan to use the pandemic as a reason to stay six feet away from people and not let anyone hold the baby. We won't go inside the trailer.

I call for directions and a man with a deep voice answers and gives me the most rez directions I've ever heard. "Under the second water tower," he says. "A white trailer near a double-wide yellow trailer. Just look for the tipi."

We drive through three trailer parks under the watchful eyes of the inhabitants and even tribal police. Nobody recognizes our car, which is too shiny to be from Pine Ridge. Everything in Pine Ridge from the cars to the broke-down trailers to the kids playing in the pot-holed streets is covered in a fine layer of dirt and dust. I know we don't fit in at all—red-on-the-outside, white-on-the-inside. I don't mind not fitting in, but I know it makes us a target. For suspicion, for manipulation, for theft, for violence. I'm glad we left Petra and Jordan at the funeral home.

We know we find it when we see a woman and three younger men trying to put up a tipi in front of a busted trailer that has a broke-down blue car in the yard and garbage piled by the door and littering the grass. There are three young men and a short, squat woman in the front yard. They are covered in dirt and barely acknowledge us as they try to toss a thick rope over the top of a bunch of tipi poles, pitched haphazardly over each other. With each toss, they struggle to get the rope in between the right poles. I suggest a heavy item tied to the end of the rope. They don't acknowledge me. I ask where to put the food, and someone motions inside.

Logan and I grab the food and walk up the makeshift stairs into the rotting trailer. I mean *rotting* as in, the wood is rotting away. There is no carpet, no floor, just wood. No doors on the pantry shelves, where a teenager reaches up to pull out three little baggies filled with white powder. He looks at us over his shoulder, says "hey," and runs off into a back room.

I set the food on the table, where a tiny woman sits in a chair, her head lolling back. I think she's sleeping, but when I speak, her head jolts awake and her eyes lazily peel open, and then I smell the stale beer. Her pores ooze with it.

"Oh, hi . . . " she slurs. She reaches her hand out. I'm afraid to touch anything; afraid not to. I touch her palm lightly with two fingers. "I'm Bree." She fights to keep her heavy lids open.

"Oh! Aunt Bree. So nice to meet you!" And now I know why she never called me or Petra back. It had nothing to do with us. None of this has much to do with us at all.

Back outside, Logan helps the men and the one woman with the tipi. They keep throwing the rope, and it flails wildly.

"Really, you guys should tie something heavy to the end of the rope."

Nobody listens. I start searching the ground for something suitable. They keep throwing the rope wildly. Logan joins in, flinging it towards the top, never in the right spot. I think about how the definition of insanity is doing the same thing over and over again, expecting different results. I find a half-drank Gatorade bottle in the car, something Logan was drinking and will probably never finish. I grab it and walk back to the tipi.

Someone swings the rope and misses again. The group's interest is faltering, I can feel it. I pick the rope off the ground and tie the Gatorade bottle to it. They all look at me. I throw the bottle. I don't have enough force, but it still almost makes it.

Now they see what I'm doing. I tell one of the taller guys to throw it. He does, and he makes it. The energy around the group changes, becoming more active, palpable, excited, hopeful. They ask me who I am. I tell them.

All of a sudden, they see me. They introduce Logan and I to our grandkids. I think they are technically our second cousins, but Lakota-way, they are our grandkids. One is three years old—Acacia's age—and one is six—a little older than Aurora. I forget their names in the shower of other names I hear that day, but I remember DeMarcus, the little one, the one they call Squeaks. He keeps staring at me like he doesn't know if he can trust me. His little bare feet scamper over the garbage.

My phone buzzes with a text against my hip.

Are you on your way back? It's been a half hour.

And another one a few minutes later.

Don't LEAVE me here!

I explain to my new relatives that we need to go back to the funeral home to get my sister, but we would be back shortly.

At the funeral home, we find Bree talking to Petra. I hadn't even noticed she left. She smells of beer still. At least she seems more lucid.

They ask us to approve the little paper funeral handouts, which feature an eagle in front of a 70s-style dreamcatcher on the cover, above script letters spelling out "In Loving Memory." The inner verso page features a random Christian-inspired poem called "Safely Home" that I skim over. I don't care for it, but how would I know what my birth father would have liked? I barely knew him. On the recto, it states:

In Loving Memory of
Edwin Francis Blackfeather
Date of birth   Date of passing
October 18, 1950 – August 27, 2020
Pine Ridge, SD   Lake Park, IA

Wake Services
3:00 P.M. Thursday, September 3, 2020
Trisha Wilds Residence
Pine Ridge, South Dakota

Funeral Services
10:00 A.M. Friday, September 4, 2020
Trisha Wilds Residence
Pine Ridge, SD

Officiating
Sister Nancy Schneider

Traditional Lakota Services
Mr. Yamni Clear Water

Pallbearers
Jadan Poor Bear   Francis Poor Bear   Daniel Poor Bear
Aaron Poor Bear   Dakota Wilds   Darien Hill

Honorary Pallbearers
All Friends & Relatives

Graveside Services
Our Lady of the Sioux Catholic Cemetery
Oglala, South Dakota

The backside lists the surviving family members, featuring Petra, Sid, me, and Levi. At the bottom of the page, the family members who have preceded him in death are listed.

After looking it over, we nod our approval. They ask if we would like to see the body while they make copies. Petra and Bree and I follow a staff member into the viewing room, where the light is turned low and soft around a light-blue casket with the top portion open. The inside is lined with white silk. It's a nice coffin.

When I see him, I laugh. Petra and Bree, already sobbing, stare at me, mouths open. I can't help it. His eyes are crinkled at the edges, and his mouth is pulled into a coyote smirk. He looks like he is going to sit up any moment, say "Gotcha!" He looks like he is pulling a trick on us. I can't believe he is dead. Even in death, he looks so alive.

Something about his smile puts something at rest inside me. I feel like Eddie just shared some private joke with me. *Ha! I'm not really dead, Baby Girl. I'll be with you still.* Something in me is just convinced he's still around.

Back at the tipi, the guys unload the van with the coffin and body inside it. They place the coffin on a table set up inside the tipi, which is half-done.

A young man who introduces himself as my nephew Dakota stands next to us, holding Squeaks.

"I'm sorry guys," he whispers loudly so only we can hear. "This is shit."

"No!" we placate half-heartedly. "It's perfect."

"No." He looks at us each in turn, sternly. "It is shit." He walks off. We giggle a little bit to ourselves.

It's quite a sight to see. They made the tipi too wide with the poles spread too far apart, so when they wrapped the canvas around it, the material only made it halfway around. They tied the canvas halfway around the poles and called it good. They left the Gatorade bottle tied to the rope, which was dangling over the body once it was set inside. Someone tried to make it look nice by putting some fleece blankets in Southwestern patterns over two tables on either side of Eddie. The funeral staff set a sign-in sheet and the handouts with the tacky eagle and dreamcatcher design on one of the tables. Random people I didn't know started signing the sheet and paying their respects. There is no ceremony.

"Dakota," I say when he comes back to us with tattered chairs to sit on, "what is Squeaks' real name? DeMarcus, right?" I sit on a chair and then quickly stand back up when I realize it is soaking wet, possibly with someone's pee.

"It's . . . It's Squeaks," he says. "That's what you can call him." I wave to Squeaks, who glares me down before reaching out for Dakota again. Tough kid.

Logan and I call his brother "The Boy with the Watch." He keeps showing us, over and over, this blue-and-black watch that takes photos and that you can play games on it. He shows me how he can jump from each level of the trailer's stairs, taking a running jump from the very top stair and landing with a POOF! in the dirt. I tell him he is a daredevil. He cautiously confides in me that he has tried to jump from the roof of the trailer. I recommend he not do that if he wants to be able to jump from anything ever again. He smiles at me. I know he is going to do it again.

Aunt Maureen—a humble elderly woman hunched over a walker, her face etched with laugh and frown lines drawn like mesas—shows up. We make small talk, and I take a photo of her and Bree. Dakota comes out of the trailer with cheesecake and fruit for Petra, Logan, and me. For a minute, we enjoy the sun and the family we have never met.

I tell Petra and Logan it's time to go. They didn't seem very motivated, but I'm worried about the relatives in the trailer doing meth and the relatives in the nearby grove of trees smoking weed and the relatives in their cars drinking. It doesn't seem like a good mix, and it's almost dinnertime. I feel, in my bones, that if we stay much longer, something is going to go down. I persist until we've said our goodbyes and are safely in the car. We drive through the Badlands on the way back to Rapid, stopping at the three dead presidents carved into a mountain.

I feel rough and drained the next morning, not at all ready to bury my birth father. I down coffee as we get ready and pack the car. We plan to leave for Colorado right after the burial to take Petra home and stay the night before heading home the next morning. Logan and Petra look the way I feel, yawning and bleary-eyed.

When we get to the rez, my bladder feels like it's going to explode. Apparently, tiny bladders run in our family because Petra is also in need of a bathroom. Rather than risk a meth-ridden bathroom or squatting in the trees alongside my aunt Trisha's trailer space, we decide to stop at the funeral home before heading to Trisha's.

Once inside, a young woman meets us at the door.

"Oh, do you guys know what happened?"

Our eyes get big.

"No, what happened? At the trailer?"

"Let me get Mike."

We use the restroom while we wait.

Mike, a taller and lighter-skinned man than I expected, comes out of his office with a grave face. He plants his feet wide and claps his hands together, rubbing them while he talks.

"Okay, so. Here's the thing. They were all drunk and high down there all night, and there was an altercation, and a man died. They put him in the tipi next to your father's body." Petra and I look at each other, eyes wide, mouths open. "An ambulance went and picked him up this morning. I don't know how this happened, but someone broke the handles on the casket, and I had to go down there to fix them.

"They are saying that he died of COVID. I haven't received confirmation—the coroner is testing him now. Someone also robbed a bunch of people down there, including Maureen." I inhale quickly, bringing my hand to my mouth. "The family has asked us to put off the burial until 3 p.m. I'm not sure what to do."

Petra and I look at each other again, reading each other. I start shaking my head.

"No, no, we can't wait that long," says Petra, her voice rising.

"No, we can't," I agree. "We came all this way. I kind of just want to get the body out of there and take it to the burial site, just to get him out of that environment."

"Yes." Petra nods. "Yes, we need to get him out of there. Can we do that?"

Mike nods, slowly. His shoulders visibly relax.

"Actually, yes, I'm worried, too. And it's ultimately your decision, Petra, as the oldest, so yeah, we can get a van ready. We just need your pallbearers ready."

We assure him we can round up the pallbearers. We get in the car and head toward the trailer.

When we get there, Dakota is disheveled in a dirty yellow T-shirt, hair messy like he just woke up, holding Squeaks at the top of the stairs leading to the trailer. Logan, Petra, and I grab the food from the car and walk it over to hand to Dakota.

"Oh, shit," we hear him mumble quietly as he sets his eyes upon us. He sets Squeaks down and takes the donuts and water inside. We get more from the car and set it on the tables, which have been moved outside the tipi. Every muscle in my body is pulled taut.

When Mike pulls up with the van to get the body, Logan goes and stands with the funeral staff while everyone waits for Dakota to bring Aunt Maureen out. Our new-found cousin Jennifer asks for some sage. I get a small sage bundle out of my car and hand it to Jennifer, who lights it and starts smudging the body and the people waiting. She prays quietly.

A tall man, about sixtyish, with long, graying, dark hair, stands by the body holding a star quilt and a feather fan. He also seems to be praying. Dakota brings out safety pins with beads on them for the pallbearers; he puts one on Logan's Pendleton vest.

When Maureen comes out, her hair and clothes are messy, like she was just pulled from sleep. I think of how Mike said she had been robbed. I hug her and ask if she is alright.

"I have been crying all night," she says. "I'm all cried out."

When I pull away, I notice several large stains of blood on the bottom of her shirt and wonder whose blood that is.

Trisha stands in the doorway with Squeaks on her hip, raising her voice, repeating, "Someone is spreading rumors that blind guy died of COVID. He didn't die of COVID." Someone shushes her, and she goes back inside. I notice they are all being much better about wearing their masks today.

Mike comes over and whispers to me, "I talked to the coroner. He said the blind guy tested negative for COVID."

"Okay, thank you," I say. "But . . . so . . . he did die, right?"

"I . . . I'm not sure."

My forehead wrinkles.

"But you talked to a coroner, right?"

"Right."

"So somebody died."

He shrugs. Frustrated, I turn away. The guys are getting ready to move the body into the back of the van. I wipe down the casket with antibacterial wipes, noticing that the handles on the casket seem fine. The pallbearers pick up the body and slide the casket into the vehicle. I tell Petra to get in the car with the baby, as I head toward the car, as well. I yell back at Logan to come when he is done. I don't want to miss the line of cars to heading to Oglala, where we will bury Eddie.

The funeral van starts up as the other cars filled with relatives load up, Indians piling on top of themselves in cars and the backs of trucks.

We listen to peyote and powwow music from Pine Ridge to Oglala. I try singing along with the music, but I keep getting choked up every time I watch a car pull to the side of the highway in honor of the caravan—in honor of my birth father and our family.

We pull up a dirt path into the cemetery once we get into Oglala. It is on a small hill. We park next to the cars and trucks of my family members.

The pallbearers bring Eddie, with a closed casket, to the deep hole dug into the dirt the day before. They lay a pine box inside the hole, and then the pallbearers slowly inch the casket down into the hole, into the pine box, using a silky fabric. My husband joins them in laying Eddie to rest. Dakota jumps into the hole to nail the lid on the pine box shut.

Sister Nancy, a tiny white woman with reddish-brown bangs and hair in a ponytail, reads passages from the Bible. During the call and response portion, nobody responds. She keeps on, the hot wind blowing through her. When she asks if anyone wants to share any stories, nobody speaks.

Jennifer keeps hugging Petra and I in a way that is meant to be comforting, but we don't know her, and we suspect she was part of the group that killed a man early that morning and set him beside our father's body to die. We don't know who to trust or who to believe, so we quietly shake her off. When she walks to the baby to pick him up, Petra asks her not to. Jennifer says, "I don't have COVID, don't worry." I ask Petra if she wanted me to tell her to go away. Petra shakes her head and tells Jennifer not to let anyone else touch Jordan or even get close to him. Jennifer promises she won't. She takes him to a spot of shade. We keep our eyes on her.

Sister Nancy tells the men they can start shoveling. I walk up to the edge, pick up a handful of dirt, and throw it in. Someone hands me some sage and sweetgrass. I hand some to Petra, and we both throw in the Lakota medicines to accompany our father to the spirit world.

Nobody has done anything ceremonial in Lakota way, beyond Jennifer smudging and praying before we left for Oglala. I want to sing to him, but I am afraid I will cry, and then the song would be ruined. But I have to do something. Someone has to do something for him. In a ceremony way. I can't let him be buried without that.

What I want to sing is a Navajo prayer song I sang to my girls a million times when they were babies to put them to sleep. In a way, I would be singing him to sleep, too, and I like the idea of that. But I know I will never last through that song. So I sing two peyote songs I know. I get through two verses each before I lose it, heaving huge sobs while Petra holds me and the men shovel. I have my eyes closed the whole time I sing and cry, so everything feels dark and dreamlike. I feel arms around me and the warmth of the sun and the cool tears on my cheeks. I feel childlike and calm after the tears stop.

Sister Barb brings over a cross with a Jesus on it. It was from the front of the casket. She asks if one of us wants it. Petra grabs it right away, asking, "Can I? Do you mind?" I don't have anything of his." I don't either, but I don't have any desire for a Jesus dying on the cross, so I tell her, "Go ahead." I walk away to stand behind Logan as he shovels.

They shovel for such a long time. The wind is blowing hot air as the sun climbs higher in the sky, and my cousin Julz plays Lakota prayer songs on her phone. I watch the sweat bead along the edges of Logan's forehead and down his nose. I look down at his shoes—his brand-new fancy Italian leather shoes that cost him $150—covered in a light layer of dirt. He stops occasionally to catch his breath, but he never really takes a break. At one point, it is just him and the funeral director shoveling.

Sister Nancy comes to stand beside me, holding the star quilt my aunt gave her as payment for her service. It's the quilt they used to cover the bottom part of the casket.

"Can I help my husband?" I ask her. "Or is this, like, a guy thing I'm not supposed to do?"

"Yeah," she says. "It's definitely a guy thing. I think you'd be showing the rest of them up, and they probably wouldn't like that."

"I know, I just don't want him to have to do it by himself."

She turns to me, offering the blanket.

"I want you to have this. Your Aunt Maureen gave it to me, but I know you don't have anything from him, and I want you to have something to remember him by."

I take it and hold it to my chest.

"Thank you!" I exclaim. It is better than a cross. "Thank you." I don't know what else to say. She smiles and stands next to me in silence for a while, and then she walks away to pay her respects to my aunts. The tall older Indian guy I saw back at the tipi, the one with the star quilt and the feather fan, comes over to stand next to me. I ask him his name.

"Jack Clear Water," he tells me. "I'm your uncle. My brother is Yamni Clear Water. He was close to your dad." He tells me where he lives, introduces me to his daughter. He stands next to me, quiet and still and strong as a tree.

When the guys are finished, I tell everyone we have to go. I just want to get away from the reservation and put it all behind us. We shake hands and hug, despite COVID. I hold Aunt Maureen for a long moment and tell her I love her, and then I give her my earrings, a pair I made to match the ones I gave Petra. I tell Petra to give hers to Aunt Bree and that I would make her a new pair to replace them. Bree can barely hold them in her hand; she is drunk again, so desperately drunk.

I breathe a sigh of relief when I shut the car door.

There is a knock on the window when I start my car. Dakota. I forgot to thank him. I hug him tight and thank him for burying Eddie. We tell Dakota he needs to keep everyone straight, protect them, especially the kids. He hesitates and then agrees. I can see a struggle playing out on his face.

When we leave, I can't get out of there fast enough. Logan and Petra want to stop at the new Taco John's on the rez. I am so angry. All the anger I held at what happened during the wake bubbles to the surface as we wait in the drive through line, which extends into the street. I snap at Petra and Logan for making me stop. I just want off that awful, horrible reservation.

I drive sixty-two miles an hour until I get to the edge of the reservation, which isn't far. Then I gun it.

As I drive, putting miles between me and the reservation, I think, over and over, trying to make sense of it:

My birth father was assaulted.
He was in a coma for four months, and I didn't know it.
There was a murder this morning.
The man died next to my father's body.
Eddie is buried in Oglala, next to his parents and his brother.
There was no ceremony.
There was no ceremony.
There was.

All The Things I Know: A Profile of a Father in Vignettes

To Eddie:

You know that famous profile of Sitting Bull by the chief headdress, full of eagle feathers, two plumes dangling on either side of his face? You also know it by the curve of his nose, like it is broken in the middle, sharp slanting down like an upside-down and backwards *L*. The tip, curved under like a hook. I grew up loving and hating that nose, a lot like I have grown to love and hate you. What makes me both unique and fucked up is that I am your daughter.

When I first met my birth mother, I asked her about my dad. She said that he beat her. She kicked him out at least four times, because there are four of us. In between Sid and me, she had a psychotic break. She can't remember if she was pregnant with me when it happened. She can't remember where I was born. She only remembers dancing in a thunderstorm, in and out of a rain puddle with Petra, and me in her belly, thinking, *This is the only time we will dance together, the three of us.* She named me Raindance, but you call me Baby Girl because that's what was on my birth certificate when you learned she gave me away.

I find your sister before I find you. I met someone from Pine Ridge who knew your family, and she gave me Maureen's number. When I call, her husband says, "Someone's on the phone for you. Sounds like a white woman." His words stung. Maureen picks up the phone, cautious at first. Then she sees an opportunity. She tells me you ran off after I was adopted. She says you have land; she will help me get it when you die. Maureen asks me to see if I can get ahold of the checks the tribe is holding for you from the person that is renting your land; she thinks if you're dead, I can help her get the money. "Can you kick your auntie a thousand bucks?"

You have some kind of condition that makes you gray. Your hair and eyes and brows and lashes and skin—all gray. My adoptive mom, a nurse, tells me that's from drinking, from your liver trying to hold on. But Levi is the same color—all ash and soot, like something that used to be on fire and has long since burned out. Your hair is fluffy like mine when it dries, like you've stuck your fingers in a light socket. Your fingers, long and slender. Growing up, my grandpa grabbed my fingers as I passed by; "Piano fingers!" he exclaimed.

"Baby Girl, I wanted you. I came back for you, to try to keep you." I'm on the phone with Eddie for the first time. He says he didn't want June to have me adopted out, says he tried to get me back, but "It was already done." Later, he tells me the best thing he did was let me go (didn't he just say he didn't authorize my adoption?), so that I wouldn't know anything of our reservation. I wouldn't know the horrors my family experiences every day—until I saw it myself at his funeral.

I have a photo of the last time you and June and Petra and Sid were together. In it, you look tall, but you're only taller than the rest of them, which isn't saying much because June is so short and the kids are just kids. Petra is wrapped around your neck, her little face peeking from behind your puffy hippie hair. June cuddles Sid to her chest, a lazy grin on her face. You look like happiness, like hope. In fact, you all look like photos of my adoptive family. In a way, I got the family Petra and Sid were supposed to have.

Eddie's ex-wife Luz calls and tells me they divorced. She towered over him, but somehow, he still beat her enough to incur assault charges and flee the state. She tells me she loves me, that God loves me, that she wishes things were different, that he can't quit drinking, that she's worried for him. I'm worried for her, for the son who towers even over her whose head was bashed in by a group of boys when he raped a girl . . . whose fingers crept towards my bare legs as I sat on their couch, sweating in the heat, surrounded by cockroaches.

After you disappear, I start Googling your name periodically. Every few days, I type in "Edwin Francis Blackfeather." I just want to know if you are alive or dead. I find a photo of your tribal ID. You look puffy and sick in it, but your hair is longer, blacker, younger. It shows a Nebraska address. I find your old Nebraska address and about fifteen other addresses associated with your name, from the Midwest to the East Coast. I find a long list of criminal offenses, some recent. I wonder if anyone would tell me if you died.

For years after I meet you, after you leave Luz, I get random calls from jails, prisons, rehabilitation centers, and pay phones across the country. I learn to pick up the phone every time I get a call from a number I don't recognize. The area codes change, getting closer to the Midwest as they move from the East Coast. Our calls, our brief, but it's enough that you call me to tell me that you love me—enough that you remember my number. You ask how school is going, tell me you are proud of me. You say you want to talk to my birth siblings, too.

Levi and Eddie meet in Rapid City long after I meet Eddie in North Carolina. I help them find each other, connecting them via phone numbers. They go on a binge and beat someone up together—like father, like son. I say nothing of the thing Eddie told me after that time we shared a forty that we sneaked out of Luz's house in the North Carolina heat. Because he just said it to be mean; Levi is the only one who looks even a little bit like him.

Sid and Petra refuse to contact our father. He abandoned them. They were old enough to remember him—remember his love, remember his abuse, remember him leaving. And then everything that happened after. His leaving started a chain reaction of traumas, little and big, that happened to them growing up. Every scar is a slight against him—a tick on the counter that adds up to all the reasons they escape into sex, into meth, into a bottle. And then they abandon their children like animals, just like he did, starting the cycle all over again.

My sister Petra calls me crying, after months of us feuding over her abandonment of her children. "I never got to know him!" she wails.

My body is made of steel, cold as ice. She barely remembers him, but she has his last name, and therefore, is the only one allowed to make any decisions about his funeral, since our brother Sid is in prison. She repeats this to me, over and over, as if the repetition will wear down the metal encasing my heart. When they bury his body in the dirt, I am the one who cracks.

I friend my cousin Dakota on Facebook after your funeral, call to tell him thank you for helping bury your body. He slurs as he tells me story after story about you. "He was a pool shark, just like you," he says. "He taught me how to hustle." In Dakota's version of you, you were the patriarch of the family, the elder, the one everyone went to for spiritual advice. You were the rock, the glue holding everything together. Dakota tells me, "He taught me everything I know." And now Dakota steps up to keep it all together, "slaying dragons" at night to keep his nephew safe.

I explain to my birth mother that these are the only things I know about him. I only met him once, so I live through the stories other people have told me. She tells me he was also kind and loving, smart and entrepreneurial, driven like me. She tells me that people came to him for advice and that he had a calming and gentle way of talking to people, yet he was strong, so people respected him. She says he could hold a room, pausing, letting the air fill up and swell like a balloon before delivering the final blow.

Maybe there is more to you than I thought, more than I knew. What no one understands is that I only met you once in person. This is all I have of you—pieces of the puzzle that is a portrait of you, holes where a father should be but wasn't. I learned to be grateful for the pieces; some kids don't have even one piece to hold on to. There is one moment I remember, when you took me for a walk alone in North Carolina. We snuck beers and I felt like your son, not your daughter. We sat on an old, broke-down truck in the middle of nowhere up in the hills and drank. It wasn't much beer, but your eyes lit up like mine do when I get that sweet relief. And then you told me your secrets in a rolling voice that reminds me of prairie, sweet and dark.

How to Fill a Hole

I remember the very first game of pool I played competitively. A woman on my mom's league, Tammy, didn't feel like playing and asked me to step in.

Tammy was tall, with bottle-red hair, light, papery skin, and nice makeup with muted red lips and dark mascara. Her voice was high and nasally—like a Midwesterner, but without the accent. She was very pleasant, gentle with a kind smile; however, she could glare you down across a pool table as good as any of the others on a bad night. She was a very good player—they all were. However, some nights, she just seemed a little off, a little tired, or just not in the mood to play. It was one of those nights, so she told me to sub in for her.

"Oh!" I exclaimed, surprised. "I don't have my pool cue."

My mom shoved her stick at me. "That's okay, use mine!"

"You're up." Alex, the captain, pointed her pen in my direction as she stared down the board. When I didn't move, she flicked her light eyes at me and tucked the pen behind her ear, then crossed her arms. Chastised, I stood up and approached the table.

I was playing Pam, a large woman, both in stature and girth, but most of all, in personality. It was the dead of winter and the bar had terrible heating; all of us were bundled up in hoodies and sweaters, but not Pam. Pam wore shorts and a tank top, her mane of hair pulled into a low ponytail, jewelry glinting off her fingers and ears. Her cue, with the handle carved into a spiral shape, was hot pink all the way through. Her tank top was hot pink too.

And her voice! A heavy baritone. Something deep in my gut reverberated when she said, "I'm Pam. Good luck." I felt my adrenaline spike, my heart in my throat.

As big as she was, Pam slammed the cue ball into the pack, balls careening off the rails, then slammed one after the other into the pockets. She missed, and it was my turn. It was happening so quickly, my anxious brain needed time to catch up.

I was so nervous that my cue was shaking. I took deep breaths and tried to steady my hands. I felt propelled to keep up her pace, slamming the balls around, but I knew I needed to slow myself down to think. I hadn't yet picked out which ball I was going to hit, and Pam was already sighing and stomping her feet . . . I swear I saw steam coming out her ears.

"Take your time, honey!" My mom was notorious for taking her maximum allowance of time on each shot, causing her opponent to become flustered and lose their cool, allowing her to take control of the game. She taught me how to do the same. Pool is as much a mind game as it is physical. It's like chess but with more action.

I took one shot, and it went in. I took another. And another. Then missed. We traded off like that, down to the 8-ball. It was a long shot down the rail, and she missed. I had to do a tight cut; too much angle, and I'd miss. Too little, and not only would I miss—I would also scratch, and the game would be over. I barely tapped it in, and the cue ball stayed away from the dangerous pocket. My team cheered. Even Pam clapped, laughing, and patted me on the back in congratulations. My mom hugged me.

"You did good, kid," said Alex in a low voice as she passed me on her way up to the table. I glowed from her small praise the rest of the night.

My adoptive parents met over a game of pool. They both lived in Central Oregon for a time. My mom didn't feel like going to the bar that night, but her best friend Bobby coaxed her into going out. My dad was there playing and drinking with his best friend. Bobby and my dad's best friend ended up dating for a while. My parents dated, too; they just never stopped.

For their twentieth anniversary, they bought a pool table and put it smack in the middle of our dining room—where you might expect a table for eating—right under the chandelier. It was the first thing you saw when you walked into our house. It defined my family—my parents and brother all played really well, late into the night, smoking weed and shooting.

I always felt like the black sheep growing up with them. I didn't react well to pot. I am one of those people who reacts the opposite way you're supposed to. I'm naturally a type-A personality—wound up and anxious, always with a to-do list and color-coded charts. I'm the person who needs pot the most, but it makes my anxiety worse, causing panic attacks and paranoia, instead of doing what it should.

And I didn't really like pool.

My parents bought us pool gloves and cue sticks and chalk holders and bags to hold it all for birthdays, Christmases, and even Easter. I was always disappointed it wasn't sparkly nail polish or a Coach purse. I didn't appreciate pool until I was twenty-one, hitting the bars and flirting with boys. Although I wasn't nearly as good as my parents or my brother, I could hold my own against most casual players, which impressed many cute guys. And it was something to do, something to bond over, that was a welcome relief to standard dates, where all you do is talk.

There is also something just right about watching an entitled white man fall, to have something that he can't, to prove him wrong about you, about being a woman, about being a brown woman. Justice. You can't argue a game of pool—you either win or you don't. I once admitted to my husband, drunkenly, that I love playing white men because they flatter me, flirting—which quenches my ego—and then I get to watch as their faces transform when they first realize I am a threat to their own . . . and then they shatter with embarrassment, defeated. They will come back again and again, refusing to believe that it wasn't just a fluke. I didn't just get lucky—I'm just better, and there really isn't anything they can do to change it.

When I moved back to Portland from Washington, DC, my mom invited me to come hang out at the bar with her. Her pool team was playing, and she wanted me to come watch.

"I'm so excited you are old enough to come to the bar with me now!" she exclaimed. "Now, you're not just my daughter—you're my friend."

It became our weekly routine. Every Thursday, I'd take the MAX from downtown Portland, where I lived in my off-campus apartment, to Parkrose, where my parents lived on the same street as my aunts, uncles, and cousins. We'd have a meal, either all together at my grandparents' house or just our immediate family. Then my parents and I would drive together to whichever bar my mom was playing at with her team, and my dad and I would watch, cheering her on, chatting with her teammates and their spouses and daughters. Sometimes, I would invite friends to meet me there, where we would begin our night before heading to the next venue.

One night, someone on my mom's team was sick, and they asked me to sub.

"Yeah, you know what you're doing," said Alex. Sometimes, she stayed after the games wrapped up to play a few games with me. "Just get in there and have a good time."

It started like that. Whenever someone was sick, Alex would text me and ask if I would be there. Suddenly, I realized that I was subbing every week. I overheard someone planning to take the next week off, and my mom confirmed it. They were all in on it, planning to rotate out so they all got a break.

Then, my parents moved. They bought a plot in a tiny town in Quilcene, Washington, out in the forest off Highway 101 just north of Olympia and on the way to Port Townsend. It was beautiful, nestled in between the mountains and the ocean.

"So," said Alex, about a month before the big move. "You know you're going to have to take your mom's place, right? That's been the plan all along." She smiled.

I wanted to be just like Alex. She was a badass, with a career job, an expensive pool cue, and most of all . . . a brand-new silver Mustang. Her husband had died years earlier, and she had a tough stoic presence, with a mean resting bitch face framed by silver strands and a jaw that jutted out like a boxer's. She scared me until I got to know her better.

Most of the women in the pool league scared me. Over the years, I realized these were the women I wanted to impress the most—the "mean" ones, the tough pool women who looked like they would beat you on the pool table or off for fun. I imagine I was like a little puppy, following them around, asking for advice on shooting, on men, on life.

One of the pieces of advice that stuck with me, that I've heard over and over, is that "You're not really playing your competitor—you're playing yourself. You're playing to become better than you were before." For someone like me, a perfectionist who moves on once I feel I've mastered a thing, pool is the game that keeps giving. A perfect game is so rare, even for the pros.

After a night of pool, I dream in geometry. I fall asleep going over and over the shots I made, trying different angles, speeds, strategies. After a couple days of playoffs or a long weekend tournament, I start seeing pool balls and cue sticks everywhere. A woman talking to me becomes the cue ball, and her husband next to her becomes the 8-ball, and I feel a compulsion to shove one of them into the other. I start zoning out when people talk to me, imagining shot combinations ending in the security guard being flung into the men's-restroom-sized pocket. I keep my husband up at night going over strategy he cares nothing about, and I am wide awake, staring at the ceiling, a pool table flying above my eyelids.

"You play pool?"

I'm on the phone with my cousin Dakota in the middle of the night after Logan and I get back from burying Eddie. I've got a pretty good buzz going after four hours in the bar down the street, playing pool with the local guys. Pool is less a hobby and more a compulsion, which has gotten worse with the stress of the pandemic and my birth father's death. There is a need in me to both drink until I can't feel anything and play pool until I can no longer stand.

Dakota simply doesn't sleep at night. He lies in his car with the sleeping bag and thick jackets I sent him, cuddling Squeaks—his two-year-old nephew, my grandson—to keep him warm in the dead of winter. Squeaks sleeps out in the car with Dakota because it's safer than in Dakota's mom's trailer, where she and Dakota's brother stay up all night, tweaking. Dakota doesn't sleep so he can keep Squeaks safe.

One night on the phone with Dakota (not this particular night), his brother came home swinging a bat and yelling at Dakota to come out and fight him. I heard Dakota yelling, and then I heard scuffing, and then running and breathing, and then *bang bang bang* . . . and then silence. I tried all night to get ahold of Dakota. He called me the next morning and explained that his brother—in a tweaker blackout—had beat him up with a baseball bat, and he ran away from the car to keep his brother away from Squeaks and called the police. The police came and picked up Dakota's brother.

Dakota and I talk frequently in the middle of the night, usually drunk, keeping each other company, not letting each other feel so alone.

"Your dad was a pool shark," Dakota announces, with a laugh. "I play some, too. We used to hustle white boys at the pool hall. I guess it's in your nature then."

Persian people—like many cultures—insist that we developed astrology. There is something to it all . . . I mean, consider the moon and its pull on women, causing our bodies to sync with the bright orb in the night sky, the ocean waters, and each other. If the moon can do that, it is plausible the stars have some kind of effect on us all. I'm sure there is more science behind all of this, but I don't know it.

I subscribe to Astrology.com. I don't pay anything for it; I signed up in college, before they charged subscribers, so I keep receiving daily emails without having to pay. My daily astrology update gives me a page-long breakdown of my day, including career, financial, and love spotlights. Most of the time, it's vague enough that it could apply to just about anything. However, sometimes, it's uncannily spot-on.

I'm a Cancer. More specifically, I am a Cancer-Gemini cusp, with a Leo moon and a Capricorn rising. This means that I am emotional, empathetic at my core, and love to socialize and have deep conversations. I am both loyal and flighty, flitting from person to person, activity to activity. I like to try new things and places and events, but I crave structure and family.

To the public, I am a social butterfly, attention-seeking, and arrogant, the life of the party. At work, I'm hardworking, demanding, bossy, direct. You don't really see the emotional core of me, the part that is soft and fragile —the Cancerian—until you get to know me. Cancerians are crabs—we hold our softness inside a tough outer shell. It takes years to truly get to know us.

My husband is a full-on Cancer, right in the middle of the sign. Same with our oldest daughter. Acacia, the youngest, is a Scorpio—also a deep, emotional water sign. All of us need the safety and security of home.

Cancerians and Geminis are both notorious for addictive behaviors, whether it is food or alcohol or running or drugs. Whatever we are into, we want it all the time, and we go overboard. We surround ourselves with it, make it a lifestyle. Whatever it is, we are absolutely obsessed with it.

My obsessions are connected by their ability to transport me to another world, give me the ability to be someone else, to step away from my life and into another. They include reading, writing, alcohol, and pool. In some way, I've inherited all of these from both nature and nurture, from both my birth family and my adoptive family. I engage into escapism via these portals, and the rest of the world falls away. They fill me up, make me forget. But pool is my greatest obsession.

My pool idol is Jeannette Lee, the Black Widow. I have watched hours and hours of her professional 9-ball matches. I've watched her play, met her, taken selfies with her, had her sign my pool cues. I've also read her book, *The Black Widow's Guide to Killer Pool.*

It's not that it's an amazingly written book—it's that it's only one of two books I've found written by a woman about pool. (The other is Heather Byer's memoir, *Sweet*, which is now out of print.) In her book, Lee describes how she grew up with scoliosis, but wanted to be the best pool player in the world. She practiced for hours and hours almost every night in her late teens and early twenties. Her pool friends even had to take her to the hospital because she played until she couldn't walk. But she did become the best pool player in the world for eight years running, even after marriage and several children.

I'm no Jeannette Lee, but I've played as many as thirty games in a row in a night, man after man lining up to put their name on a board or quarters on the table for a chance to try to break my streak, take me down. Sometimes a woman will join in, but it's rare. When she does, I play her in a different way, like we are old friends, sisters, not enemies. We clutch hands and laugh, buy each other drinks, step out in the middle of the game to have a cigarette, leaving all the men waiting for us. On the rare moments we have control of the table, we like to make sure they know it's ours.

Recently, one of my guy friends brought a female pool player to come meet me at our local tavern. He knew we'd hit it off. She reminds me of Alex—same silver hair, similar sports car, mean RBF, and ice-cold exterior. We play about equally, trading off wins. Sometimes, she has a bad day, and I can beat her more than she beats me; sometimes, it's the opposite. Her name is Jessie, and I love playing her, always asking Troy when Jessie will be back in town.

One night, we were playing on one of the two tables in the bar. The guys next to us started bitching about having to share the less-desirable table. Jessie and I staunchly ignored them.

One of the old guys watching us from the bar counter turned around and said, "Boy, these ladies are playing better than all y'all over there . . . until you can play like them, you go on and stay at the kiddie table. This is more interesting to watch than you guys." We didn't have any trouble the rest of the night.

Every year in March, there is a ladies' invitational pool tournament in Long Beach, Washington. For one whole weekend, Friday to Sunday night, female pool players take over the Long Beach Tavern downtown and duke it out for the grand prize of a few hundred bucks for a team of five. It isn't about the prize purse, though . . . it's about owning a space that is only for female pool players, once a year, throwing down and partying it out.

The first year I went to the Long Beach tournament, I played on Lori and Kelly's team. I had been begging Diane, our local women's league owner, to help me find a team that needed a player. Lori and Kelly lost a teammate, so they asked me to fill in. Initiation involved them pouring shots down my throat all weekend and screaming at me over the pool table to "Get it together!" I learned that the only way to play that drunk and hungover and tired was to drink more.

That Sunday morning, I downed three Bloody Mary's before my match just to get up the energy to play. Everyone on my team except one sweet, quiet woman from Vernonia named Laura went outside to smoke, thinking they had time before I got to the end of my game and needed them. I lined up to break and sunk in the 8-ball. Laura and I shouted and hugged—with the 8-ball on the break, I won the match outright. An 8 on the Break is rare; everyone has a special way they break in search of it. Everyone missed it but her.

Mostly, I was grateful I didn't have to play an entire game. We had been drinking hard to power through game after game all weekend, some matches not ending until well after 1 a.m., nearing closing time, only for us to wake up at 6 a.m. for an 8 a.m. match. We came in third that weekend, and we were simply happy not to have to play the last match Sunday evening, which we heard went until midnight. Some people had to be at work Monday morning, me included.

In my early twenties, it was alright enough that I drank so much, because everyone my age did. I've never really been a fan of going out to sit around and drink and talk. When people invite me out to the bar, my first question is "Do they have a pool table?" I don't care so much about the company; as long as I have a table near, I know the night will be worthwhile.

Once, I worked with a person who was very upset by my pool playing. "Can't we ever go out just to hang out, Leah?" they asked, annoyed. I looked at them quizzically, then bent down to take my shot.

And because I'm in a bar all evening playing pool, I end up drinking. Back in my twenties, it was just what we did. I never drank soda, but in a bar, my drink of choice was a Jack and Coke. In my thirties, I graduated to just straight Jack or a dirty martini. Mid-30s, post-diabetes diagnosis, I alternate between sipping a White Claw and water; if I want to go crazy, I drink vodka sodas (no carbs) or dirty martinis (very low carb). If my girls and I want to be fancy, or if I'm at a happy hour with my coworkers, I have a tasteful glass or two of wine.

It wasn't always like that, and my responsible approach to drinking is new. After my birth father died, I was drinking so much and so quickly that, on the drug Metformin for diabetes, I was blacking out. Before Metformin and before my birth father's death, I had only ever blacked out once. It took a handful of blackouts within the year after Eddie's death for me to realize I just cannot drink like I did before.

During one of those blackouts, a girl in her twenties that I didn't know hit me in the chest at a bar while I was playing pool, and I responded with punches to her face while blacked out. Another time, a guy I thought was a friend offered to drive me home and kissed me and stuck his fingers in me after I told him several times "No."

I no longer give my guy friends a ride home, and I don't drink too much to drive myself home unless I'm with my female friends and one of them is driving us. Now I have rules and bedtimes, like Cinderella.

It took all those things to wake me up. I feel like the last year, I've been in a pandemic daze, a fog of emotional pain I kept burying or running from with alcohol or pool or books.

If I'm being completely honest with you, I always have that pain. It increases with trauma. It's like a constant wound that never completely heals, like the ankle I fractured in soccer that I never recovered from. It gets better, but something always happens, like tripping over a high crack in the concrete or jumping off something and landing on it the wrong way, or running at all, even a little bit. I reinjure it, and then I need to baby it for a while until it heals again. But it's always a bit weaker than the other ankle.

Every time I get hurt emotionally, or the rug gets pulled from underneath me, there is a pain in the middle of my chest that tears open again, and I'm raw. Like one too many Indian burns, soon even the slightest touch feels like intense pain.

I can't remember a time when I didn't have that feeling in me. It's not always so bad, but it's always there. If I think about it, I can feel it. Right now, it's buried pretty deep, not so raw. But I can feel it in the core of me still; I always have, and I always will.

Drinking numbs it so that I feel like what I imagine it would feel like if I could feel true, uninhibited joy. The best feeling is that adrenaline junkie high I get from playing pool or hiking a mountain or standing on the edge of the manmade waterfalls in downtown Portland across from the Keller Auditorium. I imagine that's how my brother, Ben, feels when he stands at the top of a mountain of snow before snowboarding down it, or before he drops into the bowl at the concrete skatepark down the street. Or how Logan felt before he jumped out of an airplane once when he was a teenager.

Those of us who grew up as kids with holes in our chests know exactly what I'm talking about. You have to find ways to fill it, so it doesn't consume you.

The cue ball drags itself down the length of the table, lightly tapping the 8-ball, which takes its time in a lazy roll, slowing as it approaches the corner pocket.

We all pause—my mom, mid-crouch, holding her stick, frozen in the same position she was in when she hit the cue ball; my dad, holding his cranberry mocktail to his chest, one arm crossed over the other, legs crossed too, leaning against my couch; me, standing kitty-corner from my mom, ready to pounce if the 8 doesn't quite make it. We all hold our collective breath.

It's just after lunch on a Sunday at my house. My parents have spent the weekend with my daughters and I, and they are getting ready to leave.

"Just one more game," my mom says. My dad, a man-on-a-trip, sighs. "Fine, but you better beat me quick, honey." Sometimes I don't know if she's here to visit me or the pool table, the one they got for their anniversary and gave to me because they wanted a real living room, instead of a pool table room.

The 8-ball teeters just on the edge, rocking gently back and forth . . . then leans in forward, just enough . . . and *plop*! She won.

When they leave, my daughters play with the balls, pulling them out of pockets and lining them against the rail.

"Mommy?" asks Aurora, who is just barely tall enough now to see over the table. "Can you show me? Can I try this?" She reaches for my cue stick but stops just short of picking it up. My daughters know enough to respect my cue sticks.

I pause, meeting her eyes. I assess her, wondering if she is mature enough to learn. Her gaze meets mine, and despite her stature, levels it.

"Sure." I pick up the cue and motion to her to join me at the table. I figure it's never too early to teach her a skill that will fill her.

What You Need to Survive

Almost every day begins with one of my daughters crawling into bed with me, curling around the warmth of my chest, head burrowed into my neck, feet tucked in between my legs where it is warmest.

Our house gets very cold at night. Logan is supposed to fix the thermometer on the heating element of our central heat system, but it seems to get knocked lower and lower on the "honey-do" list every week. I usually wake up with one child balled up inside the comma of my body and one, Aurora, big spooning along the length of my spine.

We wake up giggling and cooing or singing, bumping against Logan, who curls into a tighter ball around his slowly decreasing side of the comforter and groans. We tickle and cuddle him until he wakes.

Then breakfast. I get myself and the girls dressed while the sausages warm in the oven—two for each of us. Brush teeth and hair. Pancakes with syrup—two for me and Aurora, one for Acacia. Logan eats gluten-free cereal. I make my coffee to take upstairs to my office.

Every time I go up to my office, my daughters shout "Hug! Kiss!" and come barreling at me as I try to hold my cup stable. We perform this ritual every time I come down for a break or food or to have a conversation with Logan or to run an errand. Maybe eight times a day.

I hold my youngest, Acacia, and rock her almost to sleep every naptime or bedtime while singing nursery rhymes and Native ceremony songs. She demands I sing to her. When Logan puts her to sleep, he reads both girls a book and then sends them straight to bed. Acacia pulls a blanket to the door and whimpers on nights he puts her to sleep until either she falls asleep or one of us takes pity on her and puts her back to bed.

I once read about a study that found that every person needs at minimum twelve hugs a day to survive.

When Logan and I first got together, still practically kids ourselves, he constantly hung on to me, like a pleasant and comforting growth on my body. In all our early pictures, we are touching.

After our separation five years into our marriage, we slowly drifted apart both physically and emotionally. We rarely touched or hugged.

After we came back together and had our daughters, we attended a couples retreat during which we learned about our love languages. My primary love language is physical touch.

I thought that the reduction in physical touch in our relationship was due to the separation. As time went on, and after the couples' retreat, I started to realize that Logan grew up without a whole lot of physical touch. It was his norm to not touch or be touched. Even after we were back together and things had improved, he never really made an effort to connect physically, other than sex. I also realized that throughout our marriage, he was depressed. His normal, everyday self was sad and lonely.

I remember the day I started intentionally hugging him twelve times a day. At first, he thought it was ridiculous. He even fought it. He laughed it off like a joke. Over time, he started accepting it, quietly hugging back, but barely. Now that our daughters are three and five, I regularly encourage them to hug him with me and on their own. I know it's not really on them to give their dad affection, but I know he won't ask for it or insist on it for himself. I've raised them to be physically affectionate and encouraged them to initiate physical affection with their father. I don't know how this is going to play out in their intimate relationships later in life; however, I feel like it can never be a bad thing to be affectionate with those you love and generous in your affection.

Recently, I noticed Logan initiating physical touch more often. When our daughters demand to be hugged, when they are crying and in need of comfort, he still rolls his eyes, but he comes over and hugs them.

He's started to come over in the mornings, while I'm making our breakfast or my coffee, wrapping his arms around my waist and pressing his face into my hair, inhaling.

"You smell like a desert flower," he tells me.

I tell him I need touch to survive. I grab his hand when we are cuddling on the couch and ask him to rub my head or my back or the place on my wrists that hurts from tendonitis. When I have period cramps, I become the big spoon so I can press my belly against the warmth of his back. He's so warm, like a heater. It's become our habit to cuddle on the couch and watch serial killer thrillers while I nap in the cocoon of his warmth.

When we first started dating, he felt safe. I was a wild, hurt thing, but all I wanted to do was sleep against his body. I cried when he had to go to work. All of that went away when we separated. Now, we are journeying back to the center of us, where everything is calm and safe, and we are loved and touching.

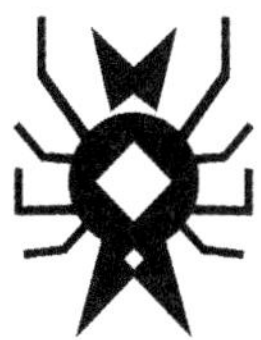

Manifestation of Our Wildest Dreams

In late April 2021, your father and I were attending a virtual training for a pool league we are trying to start in our small town (not an easy feat during a pandemic). Toward the end of the week, we both started feeling a little out of sorts. It was allergy season, so we chalked it up to that. I got better; he didn't.

What started as allergy symptoms quickly morphed into a full-blown cold. Then, it turned into something else, something worse. He couldn't get out of bed without wheezing, and he turned white and got dizzy when he tried to walk up or down the stairs. We took him to urgent care one morning; they tested him, and he came up positive for COVID. They checked his vitals and sent him home with a heart rate monitor.

At that point, we were trying to keep you girls separate from him in the hopes you wouldn't get sick. One day, you both had the sniffles; Acacia took a longer-than-usual nap, but by the evening, she was fine.

I was reading Aurora a book in bed when I noticed that she felt a little warm. Immediately concerned, I went to the bathroom to get the electric thermometer. Her temperature read 104.2—very high. I checked it again and again, but it remained between 103 and 104. I gave her some children's Tylenol and called my mom, an RN for thirty years.

"Well, she could be warm from cuddling with you and being under the covers," she said, in a soothing voice. "Give it an hour and then sneak up there and take her temperature while she's sleeping and see if it's any better."

Panicked, I cleaned the entire kitchen and sanitized all the doorknobs and surfaces in the house, covering everything in a fine layer of Lysol. Our house smelled like a hospital.

When I checked Aurora's temperature again, it was down to ninety-seven. It took me hours to go to sleep, the adrenaline coursing through my body.

You girls were fine. Nothing else happened that entire bout of COVID. At least, neither of you showed any symptoms.

It was different for your father. He got sicker, and we had to take him to the hospital. He was so pale and weak.

My automatic reaction when someone is in crisis is to get really calm and stoic. I channel my mother in her approach as a nurse. There is some emotional distancing involved. I can come off as cold, uncaring, because I don't panic or cry, or show any other type of emotion, in front of people.

Your father doesn't appreciate this aspect of my personality. The whole time I was preparing him for the hospital, driving him there, and checking him in, I was cool and collected, chatty, peppy even. It was my way of trying to keep his spirits positive. The truth is, the way he slumped in the passenger seat, his face gray, his skin smoldering to the touch . . . I had to act like someone else, like this was happening to someone else, in order to keep it together.

When we pulled up to the curb, some nurses came out to get him. They wouldn't let me even come in.

I drove home in shock, no music or podcast, no radio. Just silence. I came home and put you two to bed and then drank a bottle of wine while I talked to my best friend on the phone, crying and feeling like I couldn't breathe.

Logan was in the hospital for a week on oxygen and taking the COVID medications. I didn't have much PTO from work, and what I had, I wanted to save in case the rest of us got sick, so I just worked through it. Aurora wasn't old enough for kindergarten, and the daycares were closed, so I had to manage two young children home alone while trying to attend work meetings via Zoom and write nonprofit grant proposals. All while wondering if my husband would live.

Logan texted throughout the day most days. The worst days were the ones in which I didn't hear from him. I panicked at night, after keeping my face calm all day for my daughters and my coworkers, calling my friends and my mom, crying hysterically. I was sure I would become a single mother.

We were so lucky that he was one of the ones who got better. They let him go when he started getting bored, flirting with the nurses and causing trouble. One day, he woke up, unhooked the oxygen and monitors, and informed them he was leaving that day. After some tests, his doctor reluctantly discharged him, after making your dad promise he would take it very easy at home.

And take it easy, he did. He set up in our bonus room with the big screen LED TV. Since he couldn't leave the room except to use the bathroom, I had to make all his meals and bring them up to him. I kept you girls separated downstairs and kept you away from the bathroom he was using. Once he started feeling better, he was happy as a clam, binge-watching his favorite shows and playing video games.

Logan had to isolate for another two weeks after he got home from the hospital, so I was doing double duty on my own for a full month. My mom came several times to help with you girls, but it was still hard in between. My house was a mess, my hair was a mess, my life felt a mess, but we survived. Your dad got better, and I was relieved. I knew he was better when he dragged our washing machine out into the front yard from the bottom-floor bathroom all by himself.

When he first got out of the hospital, I told him the machine wasn't working, and I was just going to buy a new-to-us (used) machine and have it delivered and replaced, the old one hauled away. I just thought that's what you do when an appliance isn't working.

But Logan grew up differently. He grew up learning from his father and his grandfather how to fix things. He acts like it isn't a big deal, but to me, he is magic. If something is broken, he just figures it out and fixes it, when I would have thrown it away.

In this case, with the washing machine, he didn't even tell me he was going to fix it. We argued about it for a couple of days. He wanted to fix it, but I wanted him to rest. So, he snuck downstairs one day when I was taking a shower.

As I dried myself with a towel and slathered on lotion, I heard some concerning banging. Once I was dressed, I headed downstairs to see what was going on. By that point, he already had the washer outside in the grass and was sitting on the side of the porch, panting, face pale.

"What are you doing?!" I yelled. He couldn't catch his breath to answer. I made him sit and relax for a while before tearing it apart. When he did, he pulled baby socks out of the pump and installed a new one.

"Ha!" he exclaimed, pulling out the baby socks with pliers and holding them in the air, triumphantly. "I knew it. Baby socks. These things can ruin a machine." Where he heard about baby socks in washer pumps is beyond me.

I helped him move the washing machine back into the house.

We joke that Logan's spirit animal is a donkey. He is stubborn and resistant to being told what to do. However, he did get that washer working again in a weekend, saving us over $600 plus installation, just days after his quarantine period was up.

We were careful for about a month or so afterward, but we had to start doing pool tournaments to recruit players for our league. We decided it would be best for me to conduct the tournaments, since Logan wouldn't be able to get his vaccine until ninety days after hospitalization. I already had mine by that point, so I was good to go. So we thought.

I ran the tournaments for a couple months on my own while he took care of you girls. Everything was working fine; he would prep all the materials for me beforehand, and we would talk through situations that came up during the tournaments having to do with the rules or how to deal with issues with players. We started doing two tournaments a week—one on Tuesdays, and one on Thursdays. I was having the time of my life, completely in my element, until I got sick.

I ran a 9-ball tournament out of the Columbia Tavern, just down the street from our house. Every Tuesday night, I set up a tournament bracket in the bar, took an $8 buy-in from each of the players, and set up matches.

One of the regulars, Charlie, came in with a terrible attitude one night. It wasn't like him. He was normally a jolly kind of guy, everybody's friend, a peacekeeper when arguments broke out. But I even butted heads with him in a match in which I played against him and won.

"Hey!" he reached over and shook his index finger in my face. "Why don't we call pockets in these tournaments? We do that in the local league. I think we should have to call pockets."

I rolled my eyes. "That's just how we do it in our league, Charlie, you know that."

"Well, I don't like it."

"Okay, duly noted."

Later, he apologized by sharing a bite of one of his chicken strips. I hesitated, but didn't want to offend him, so I took a bite.

Two days later, I had a terrible cold. Four days later, I tested positive for COVID.

I am looking out the window that faces the ravine behind our house. I am isolated in the TV room on the second-story floor.

I love this room, and I love it even more in quarantine. The thing that made me fall in love with this house when I first saw it was the light. There are huge windows in every room and skylights in the hallway and rooms upstairs. The windows in the back face out onto the ravine, part of which we own. Our land extends down the side of the ravine to meet our neighbors' land down at the bottom, where deer play, growing little families of their own.

I've never been a birder, but I find myself staring out my office window, caught by the beauty of the light that hits the wet leaves in the spring and the snow on branches in the winter. I listen to the songs and calls of the rural birds that are much wilder and more beautiful than the city sky-rats I grew up with. I often catch a streak of red or yellow or green among a small mass of soaring brown, gray, or blue and wonder what I am looking at, a name for that wonderous sound I'm hearing.

When I start panicking about the catch in my breath, the palpitations in my chest, what my girls are going to go through if I die, I close my eyes and listen to the birds. Open the blinds on the windows facing the street and let the light stream in, basking in the sun's warmth across my face, soaking up that vitamin D. I read that people with COVID have shown lowered levels of vitamin D, so maybe infusing myself with it will help me heal.

The windows all over the house are open because of the August heat. I can hear my daughters playing, fighting, crying. I spend long moments throughout the day listening to their voices with my eyes closed.

I perk up when I hear them close by, as the light is changing to dusk. I pull my aching body up off the air mattress and go to the seat I've set up at the window so I can see them and call to them when they are playing outside. I look across the porch area and see my daughters in the window of my eldest's bedroom.

"Mom!" she calls. "Will you sing us a song? Will you sing win-day-ah-ho?"

I sing as long as I can to the air between us. She can't see the tears streaming down my face. I'm scared every day this will be the last time I get to sing to my daughters. For that reason, I sing until I feel dizzy and weak.

"I love you, Aurora! I love you, Acacia!" I wave.

"Y'uve you!" calls Acacia. I watch her little head disappear.

Aurora stands at the window, her waving hand slowing and stopping on the glass. We both put our foreheads on the window and kiss it. I slide to the floor and close my eyes. I don't even have the strength to walk to the bed.

Later that night, I wake up to the darkness and a chorus of crickets. It's 3 a.m. and I'm wide awake. My sleep schedule is out of whack from the illness and the isolation. I sleep when I get weak throughout the day and wake up at night to put my dishes in the dishwasher downstairs.

I wear an N95 mask and use disinfectant wipes to open doorknobs and touch surfaces, wiping everything down as I go. I am quiet so as not to wake anyone. "Ninja mommy," I whisper to myself. I remember sneaking out of Aurora's room as a baby after setting her down so slowly and softly, barely breathing, sometimes not breathing at all, doing a small happy dance in the hallway after closing the door if I made it without waking her up.

Moonlight streams through the skylights as I make my way down the hallway in the blue-tinted darkness with a stack of dishes and bag of garbage. I read something about a meteor shower earlier. I wonder at the stars as I tiptoe down the stairs.

After gently setting my dishes in the dishwasher my husband unloaded earlier, I wander outside. I feel a strong urge to break the barrier of my confines and experience an illicit moment of freedom.

As I walk down my patio, the concrete still warm from the daytime heat, I look up at the stars. Everything is so dark and clear; I'm surprised at their glittery brightness. A strong desire to lie on the warm earth under this sparkling canopy rises in my chest. I let myself drop to the grass.

At first, everything spins with COVID-induced vertigo, but then the sky slowly rights itself. Everything feels foggy, dreamlike. I focus on the stability of the ground beneath me, the beauty of the stars, and the wonder of the cricket songs, rising and falling in unison. I close my eyes, and it feels like the environmental elements around me are holding me, comforting me, telling me that this is what is real, and there is nothing to be afraid of, as it is all just a part of life.

I wake an hour later, startled. I don't immediately recognize where I am. The light is barely beginning to peak over the horizon, turning one end of the sky a rosy glow. I rush back inside, quietly but quickly retracing my steps. I return to my isolation room, leaving the windows open and piling blankets on my body so I can listen as the crickets tire and drop off.

The moment my quarantine is up, I talk Logan into taking us to the beach.

"I need to breathe the fresh air and feel the ocean," I say.

I take every moment I can to hug my children, to kiss their hair and squeeze their little, wriggling bodies. We chat excitedly on the drive there. Talking and sitting upright tires me, and I switch out with Logan so I can sleep a little. I've never slept this much in my life; my body cannot seem to get enough rest, like gulping water when your throat is parched.

When we get there, I keep getting out of breath walking in the sand toward the water. I have to stop and sit down frequently. It takes me several stops to make it to a good stopping point. Logan carries my bag. He is also still experiencing weakness from long COVID.

We sit on a towel back-to-back as the girls scamper off to the water. We are both completely wiped out from the walk. We breathe deeply as we catch our breath.

Logan sticks out his closed fist towards me. I bump it with my own.

"We made it," he says, still breathing heavily. I know he doesn't just mean the walk down to the beach.

"Yes, we did."

I hear him whisper, "Battle buddies."

We sit, not talking, just breathing and watching our daughters' joyous play. The wind blows through us, cleansing us, bringing us back to center.

When your father and I first started dating, we talked about whether or not we wanted children.

"I'm too selfish to have children," I laughed, sipping my drink.

Logan raised his eyebrows and nodded. "I'm deathly afraid of babies. If you had a baby, you would have to take care of it. I could take over when it's a kid." He leaned back, arms across his chest. "I don't even know how to hold a baby. The thought of it scares me. Playing games, going to movies, going skating . . . those are all fun things I'm good for. But not babies."

"Yeah," I agreed. "I could do the baby years, and then you take over for the kid years to give me a break, and then we will both have to trade off to get through the teenage years." We both paused, reflecting. "But we could do it."

"How many would you want?"

"Hmm . . ." I set my chin in my hand, thinking. "I've always wanted four, like how it would have been with my birth siblings, if I were raised with them."

"*Four?* I was thinking two."

"We could compromise on three."

"Yeah, okay. Maybe three. But let's just do two and see how it goes. I think two would be perfect, because then we each can handle one on our own."

"Yeah, we'll see."

We have had this same conversation multiple times through the years. But we never understood exactly what it meant to *be* parents. We aren't the type of people who are supposed to be good parents. We are both selfish and come from lifetimes of trauma. We both have big dreams of careers and businesses and traveling and money—none of which are quite in alignment with our dream to be parents. We also never felt like parenting was exactly our calling, until we found each other again. Before then, we didn't even try to think we could have a healthy, loving relationship and family.

Your father and I are not the kind of people who are supposed to make it as a couple. Statistically, the odds are against us. Our affinity for independence, our resistance to control, our stubbornness, our lack of skills in relationships . . . our oppositional defiance, our pain, our unhealthy behaviors . . . our brokenness, our humanity. What has kept us together, striving forward as a unit, is our mutual desire to experience a family of both nature and nurture. One that we chose, one that we created, together. Unlike our career and financial goals, we didn't even know we wanted to be parents. That dream manifested when we realized our potential together, as a unit.

We have found that in you.

Epilogue

I screamed and dropped my cell phone.

"Shit!" I exclaimed as I reached down to pick it up off the small wooden porch outside the tiny home I was staying in, while keeping my eyes on the thing that startled me in the first place—a gigantic, furry spider the size of my palm. It had skittered onto the light gray concrete at the bottom of the porch steps while I finished my cigarette, talking to my mom on the phone.

I put the phone back to my ear.

"Mom," my voice was shaky. "There is a *huge* spider next to my porch. What do I do?"

I couldn't leave it out there to sneak in through the cracks I had seen around the doors to the tiny home. While the homes were pretty decent for my rez, they weren't built to the very best standards, not like what I'd see back home in the city.

I ended up running back inside and grabbing a broom, all while talking to my mom, close to tears. I hated, hated, *hated* spiders, and this was the biggest I had seen outside of a zoo or some other contained area.

Once back outside, I sucked in my breath and dashed down the stairs before I could talk myself out of it. The spider didn't move, seemingly transfixed on the outer wall of the tiny home. I slammed the brush end of the broom down repeatedly, jabbing at the spider quickly and forcefully. It came apart, its body tearing into pieces that smeared all over the light-colored concrete. In the end, I was surprised at how easy it was.

Once I was done, I finally took another breath. I didn't even realize I had been holding it. But then, I turned and saw what the spider had seen.

There were three large black spiders. They were smaller than the gigantic spider I had just killed, but they were still large spiders. Black widows. They ran as I came at them with the broom. I killed two of them, but one got away, hiding further under the back porch area at the other end of the tiny home.

When I described the bigger spider to the tiny home rental manager, she explained that it was a wolf spider. Apparently, they are not dangerous to humans; they just look scary. In fact, you want them around, because they hunt black widow spiders, which are very dangerous to humans. They are called wolf spiders because they are solitary hunters, doing most of their hunting at night.

While spider season was ending and the manager had just sprayed the tiny home before I arrived, there was still an infestation of spiders under both porches and in the crawl space under the home. I spent the next several nights looking under furniture and behind curtains for black widows and the spiders that hunt them. I found many carcasses and a couple small live house spiders. One morning, I found a live widow in the shower.

I nicknamed the tiny home "the spider cabin."

It reminded me of my hemblecha all those years ago, in a spider den.

I was occupying the tiny home during a two-week writing residency with the new Oglala Lakota ArtSpace—a gorgeous building created to provide a gathering space for Lakota artists. I slept in the spider cabin but spent my days occupying a studio at the ArtSpace. The community building aspect of the program was a workshop I ran with participants from the Pine Ridge Girls School, who stared at me without expression and responded to my questions with one-word answers (tough crowd; regardless, I adored them).

I was originally offered a 10-week residency in May, but Logan and I were separating and selling our home in St. Helens that spring, so I negotiated a shorter residency in October, once the girls and I were settled in our new place in Vancouver, Washington. I had also just completed my very first writing residency in Homer, Alaska that August, and I couldn't justify leaving my daughters again for so long a second time during one of the hardest years of their lives.

Just as my personal life was falling apart, my professional one was taking off. When I came back from the ArtSpace residency, I received an email from Ooligan Press stating that they wanted to publish *Cekpa*.

Just like my hemblecha in the spider den had kicked off one of the biggest transitions of my life, my spider cabin residency kicked off another, even bigger life transition.

While I was there, I took a trip to Pine Ridge, where my birth father's family is from. I tried to visit Dakota and his mom, but our paths never crossed. While I was waiting for him to show, I made a side trip to the enrollment office for my tribal ID. While I had my enrollment papers from when I first got enrolled in my twenties, I never had a tribal ID. I was always jealous when my friends showed me theirs. There is something about having a tribal ID that makes you feel legit, and I had always wanted one.

What they don't tell you until you get there is that you need a money order from the post office down the street, and then they are closed for a long lunch break midday. I ended up spending the day mostly waiting.

While I waited, I people watched on the sly. Pine Ridge reminds me of Guatemala City. People walk everywhere, pushing strollers down the street, big groups of kids kicking balls into the road, elders leaning on a younger relative on one side and a cane on the other. Despite the obvious poverty, the colors are bright, the culture is alive and dancing. You can smell fire and frying meat from pop-up vendors downside streets, and everyone says hello to everyone else, chatting away. It feels like one big family in the "city center," where everyone gathers. The streets are teeming with activity and covered in a layer of red dust, tumbleweeds blowing across the streets.

I remember the first time I touched that red dust. It was my first time in South Dakota for a ceremony with Leonard Bluehorse's family. His daughter Chikala picked me up in her truck from the tiny airport in Rapid City. As we pulled out of the airport, I asked her to pull over. I jumped out of the truck, bent down to the earth, and laid down on it, hugging it. When I got up, I was covered in red dust. I licked it. I wanted it to be in me.

"I'm home," I whispered. "I'm home!" I yelled to Chikala in the truck. She laughed that uncontrollable laughter she had, her eyes lighting up (she passed away a few years ago in a very tragic accident, a result of domestic violence). She then drove me to my Aunt Maureen's, where I first met members of my birth family.

Looking at that red dust in Pine Ridge, remembering that first homecoming, my thoughts traveled to the land, what ties us to the land of our ancestors. My father's land.

I remembered something someone once told me about probate, how land can get "tied up in probate" for years and years. After my birth father died, Petra and I never heard anything about his land, despite asking. I hadn't spoken to her for a year or so, but I heard she was doing well again. The last time I visited her, she had all her kids living with her, from little Lana (not so little anymore) to baby Jayden, then a toddler. I was proud of her and hopeful maybe we would become closer again someday, our kids knowing each other in a way we never got to.

While exploring Pine Ridge, I came upon a sign for the probate office. I went there, but the office was closed until 11 a.m. When I came back later, after obtaining my tribal ID, giving Dakota a little longer to show up, I found out that our land was indeed "tied up in probate." Because June apparently told them that she thought there might be two other siblings out there from another marriage of Eddie's, the judge wouldn't close the case until we find them. Eddie never told any of the rest of us about another marriage or other siblings; it's all based on June's recollection. I hope she's right, because they will not make a determination on our father's land until we find these supposed siblings.

In the meantime, June has cut off all contact from me. She sent a message via my aunt that she needed some space from me, stating that she was upset about *Cekpa*, without giving specifics. I shared a copy of the manuscript with her for feedback earlier that year, and apparently, she wasn't happy with it. When my grandmother was on her deathbed, she told my aunt to tell me not to come visit. When Grandmother passed, they invited me to the funeral, but for me, that wasn't the point. I wanted to see her to talk to her one last time; to tell her I loved her. I didn't want to come after the fact to provide comfort to the people who had denied it for me.

While I was in South Dakota, I did visit Levi's family, my nieces and nephews and their other aunt, Ellie. They were all so sweet and beautiful and loving and smart kiddos. It has been a blessing to see them grow up via social media and the rare gatherings when I am in Rapid.

Lana calls me, mostly asking for money—thirteen dollars to go swimming at the community center or twenty dollars for DoorDash. I can't always afford it, but I do it when I can so that she knows she is loved. She keeps me updated on that side of the family, how things are going with Petra and Sid and June.

There is love there. And there is heartbreak. Neither side of my birth family is perfect. If they had been, I never would have been adopted out. Petra and Sid and Levi would not have been in and out of foster care and now struggling with addiction and mental health. Things would be very different. None of us talk anymore.

But despite everything, I have something I didn't before, and so do you, my daughters. After all of it, we have that connection to our homeland, our cekpas. It's in the form of the enrollment papers I have hidden away with the rest of my important paperwork. I filled out the paperwork during COVID, when our tribe was offering support for the costs associated with schooling children at home. When I got your enrollment papers in the mail, I cried. It was one thing to get my own papers . . . but to know that you both will grow up never having to question your identity, your connection to our land, who you are . . . it was something I could never have expected to feel, a certain kind of peace, like my soul could finally rest. A completion. Closure.

When my birth mother cut off ties with me over this book, I considered just not publishing it. Why did I need to publish it, as long as I simply had it for my children to read one day so they know their story? Why did anyone else need to read it? Was it worth it?

I could say that I want it published for other people who have similar struggles, who have lost their connection to their culture, particularly other Native adoptees. And that would be true, but that's not the real reason.

The real reason is for me. For everything I had to go through to get my enrollment, something that most enrolled Native people get as a birthright. For everything that it took from me, everything

I lost, and everything gained. For the trauma of losing a mother, and then finding her again, just to lose her one final time. For the rejection. For the heartbreak. For the love of a very imperfect father. For all the reasons I drink, happy or sad, for all the reasons I have to hike mountains until I don't feel like jumping off a cliff. For all the ways your dad and I tried to make it work for you, and for all the reasons we decided splitting up was the ultimate act of love. For the impossible dream of being a writer.

For all the ways I am imperfect as your mother, and for all the ways I love you still. For all the times I fall, and then I pick myself back up because quitting is not an option when I have you to take care of, to be a role model for, to love.

This book is a testimony to it all.

Acknowledgments

Many hands crafted this book, not only mine. I have immense gratitude towards all who have helped in the process of its creation.

Wopila to the staff and students at Ooligan Press for believing in this book and bringing it to life. It only makes sense that I would end the journey of its creation where it began.

Wopila to the readers of my many drafts, whose eyes caught the mistakes I didn't, who filled in the blanks where memory failed, and whose gentle critique pushed me to improve with every revision.

Thank you especially to Pam Houston, my mentor at IAIA, who walked with me through the deep revision portion of the process, as well as Danielle Geller and Kimberly Blaeser.

Wopila to the women readers in my family who taught me to find joy, solace, and peace between the pages of a book, especially my mother and grandmother, who were some of my very first readers and who have spent countless hours discussing *Cekpa* and supporting my career growth.

Thank you to my parents, my coparent, and many other members of my family for taking care of my children so I can write, attend residencies and workshops, and have the space and time I need to think, heal, and dream.

Wopila to the staff and writers of Writing by Writers, Corporeal Writing, Storyknife, and IAIA. Thank you to the instructors who have guided me through various portions of the project, including Cheryl Strayed, Lidia Yuknavitch, Debra Gwartney, and many more.

Thank you to battle buddies James, Justine, and Barbara for supporting me, cheering me on, and always being in my corner.

Thank you most of all to Aurora and Acacia, without whom this book would not exist.

Works Consulted

"About ICWA." National Indian Child Welfare Association. Accessed August 8, 2024. https://www.nicwa.org/about-icwa/.

Kennedy, Elicia. "The Hidden Problem of the 'very Good' Babies, Whose Passive Behaviour Masks a New Epidemic." *ABC News*, January 3, 2020. https://www.abc.net.au/news/2020-01-03/the-hidden-problem-of-babies-born-to-meth-affected-mothers/11829668.

"Methamphetamine." Wikipedia, August 6, 2024. https://en.wikipedia.org/w/index.php?title=Methamphetamine&oldid=1238928721.

"Methamphetamine." American Dental Association, July 12, 2023. https://www.ada.org/resources/ada-library/oral-health-topics/methamphetamine.

"National Survey on Drug Use and Health." Substance Abuse and Mental Health Services Association. Accessed August 8, 2024. https://www.samhsa.gov/data/data-we-collect/nsduh-national-survey-drug-use-and-health.

"Standard DBT Outpatient Services." Portland Dialectical Behavior Therapy Institute, April 12, 2021. https://www.pdbti.org/standard-dbt-outpatient-services/.

"What Does a Meth High Feel Like?" Garden State Treatment Center, May 24, 2024. https://www.gardenstatetreatmentcenter.com/what-does-meth-high-feel-like/.

About the Author

Leah Altman (Oglala Lakota) is a Native American transracial adoptee and second-generation Persian immigrant. She has worked as a freelance journalist and editor for over fifteen years, alongside her work in fundraising and grant writing for Native and BIPOC-led nonprofit organizations serving families and the environment. Leah lives in the Pacific Northwest and is an alumni of the Institute of American Indian Arts and Portland State University's Book Publishing program. Her work has been featured in publications such as *Oregon Humanities*, *The Oregonian*, *Underscore*, and *Indian Country Today*. She is an avid pool player, bead worker, fickle hiker, fair-weather kayaker, and mama bear of two young girls.

Land Acknowledgment

We acknowledge and honor Indigenous communities—past, present, and future—whose land we currently reside on here at Portland State University. This includes the traditional and ancestral homelands of the Multnomah, Wasco, Cowlitz, Kathlamet, Clackamas, Bands of the Chinook, the Tualatin Kalapuya (Atfalati), Molalla, and many other Indigenous nations who made their homes along the Wimahl, Nch'i-Wána, or swah'netk'qhu (all meaning "Big River or "Great River"), also known by its colonized name, the Columbia River. Descendants of these tribes are primarily members of the Confederated Tribes of Grand Ronde, Confederated Tribes of Siletz Indians, and the Chinook Nation. We acknowledge the current and long-standing oppression faced by Indigenous peoples and recognize that we are here because of the sacrifices forced upon them. We encourage everyone to find ways to support and connect with Indigenous communities and the land itself, and to remain committed to their justice and liberation. We also encourage folks to read the PSU Conflict Resolution department's Land Conflict Acknowledgment for further learning about the history of land conflict in this geographical area.

We attribute the name of our press to native peoples in Oregon. The Ooligan (also spelled Ourigan, Eulachon, or the Saak by the Tlingit peoples) is a Chinook word for a small candlefish that is abundant in the Pacific Northwest. The nutrient-rich oil produced from boiling the fish was traded between coastal and inland First Nations all along the Pacific coast, from California to Alaska, bringing prosperity and health to native communities. These routes were known as grease trails. Gradually, the L in Ooligan was replaced with an R, giving us the sound "ooregon". This usage became the name of a place and assumed its current spelling of Oregon in the course of history. We would like to honor David G. Lewis for his contributions to the press, along with his writings in the co-authored article Ourigan: Wealth of the Northwest Coast, which informed the name of our press in 2001.

We acknowledge the lack of Indigenous and people of color representation throughout the publishing industry, both in professional positions and as authors. Our press strives to publish culturally relevant titles from our local, diverse voices in order to make literature accessible and redefine who has a place within its pages. We commit to actively creating space for and uplifting Indigenous and other diverse authors through our work, including our How To: Publishing workshop and continued community partnerships.

Ooligan Press

Ooligan Press is a student-run trade press rooted in the Pacific Northwest dedicated to cultivating the next generation of publishing professionals. We prioritize literary equity and inclusion. Ooligan strives to publish culturally relevant titles from our local, marginalized voices in order to make literature accessible and redefine who has a place within its pages.

Project Managers

Sophia Brousseau
Claire Curry
Rachael Phillips

Acquisitions

Angela Griffin
Rin Kane
Isabel Matthews
Becca Moss
Kayla Mullinax
Emmily Tomulet

Pitch Prep

Rori Anderson
Elliot Bailey
Isabel Lemus Kristensen
Savannah Lyda
Coriander Smith

Editorial

Leena Altamimi
Jordan Bernard
Tanner Croom
Marissa Muraoka
Jessica Pelton
Tate Sears

Design

Kaitlyne Bozzone
Marielle LeFave
Ariana Protsman
Laura Renckens

Digital

Chrys Buckley
Kari Olson
Mara Palmieri
Madelynn Sare
Cecilia Too

Marketing & Publicity

Eden Herzog
Yomari Lobo
Rory Miner

Online Content

AJ Adler
Cameron Grow
Jules Luck

Operations

Kara Herrera
Julia O'Malley
Haley Young

Book Production

Leena Altamimi
Rori Anderson
Elliot Bailey
DJ Borden
Chrys Buckley
Olivia Cowles
Catherine Craig
Claire Curry
Jack Davies
Ian Drazkowski
Riley Easter
Elle Edwards
Annie Egghart
Amber Finnegan
Samantha Gallasch
Olivia Germino
Noraa Gunn
Gideon Hatt
Russ Johnson
Isabel Lemus Kristensen
Miranda Kyes
Jessie Levine
Savannah Lyda
Isabel Matthews
Quentin Nall
Trang Nguyen
Dulce Nunez
Julia O'Malley
Madelynn Sare
Tate Sears
Annaliese Smith
Coriander Smith
Elizabeth Sommer
Amber Stanton